NEW ESSAYS ON THEIR EYES WERE WATCHING GOD

★ The American Novel ★

Emory Elliott
University of California, Riverside

Other books in the series:
New Essays on The Scarlet Letter
New Essays on The Great Gatsby
New Essays on Adventures of Huckleberry Finn
New Essays on Moby-Dick
New Essays on Uncle Tom's Cabin
New Essays on The Red Badge of Courage
New Essays on The Sun Also Rises
New Essays on The American
New Essays on Light in August
New Essays on Invisible Man
New Essays on The Awakening
New Essays on The Portrait of a Lady
New Essays on Native Son
New Essays on The Grapes of Wrath
New Essays on A Farewell to Arms
New Essays on Winesburg, Ohio

New Essays on
Their Eyes Were Watching God

Edited by
Michael Awkward

Published by the Press Syndicate of the University of Cambridge
The Pitt Building, Trumpington Street, Cambridge CB2 1RP
40 West 20th Street, New York, NY 10011-4211, USA
10 Stamford Road, Oakleigh, Melbourne 3166, Australia

First published 1990
Reprinted 1992, 1995

Library of Congress Cataloging-in-Publication Data
New essays on Their eyes were watching God / edited by Michael
Awkward.
p. cm.–(The American novel)
Includes bibliographical references.
ISBN 0-521-38378-1 (hb).–ISBN 0-521-38775-2 (pb)
1. Hurston, Zora Neale. Their eyes were watching God. 2. Afro-
American women in literature. I. Awkward, Michael. II. Series.
PS3515.U789T636 1990
813'.52–dc20   90-38124

British Library Cataloguing in Publication Data
New essays on Their eyes were watching God.–(The American
novel).
1. Fiction in English. American writers. Hurston, Zora
Neale, 1901–1960
I. Awkward, Michael II. Series
813.52

ISBN 0-521-38378-1 hardback
ISBN 0-521-38775-2 paperback

Transferred to digital printing 1999

Contents

v

Contents

Series Editor's Preface

In literary criticism the last twenty-five years have been particularly fruitful. Since the rise of the New Criticism in the 1950s, which focused attention of critics and readers upon the text itself – apart from history, biography, and society – there has emerged a wide variety of critical methods which have brought to literary works a rich diversity of perspectives: social, historical, political, psychological, economic, ideological, and philosophical. While attention to the text itself, as taught by the New Critics, remains at the core of contemporary interpretation, the widely shared assumption that works of art generate many different kinds of interpretation has opened up possibilities for new readings and new meanings.

Before this critical revolution, many American novels had come to be taken for granted by earlier generations of readers as having an established set of recognized interpretations. There was a sense among many students that the canon was established and that the larger thematic and interpretative issues had been decided. The task of the new reader was to examine the ways in which elements such as structure, style, and imagery contributed to each novel's acknowledged purpose. But recent criticism has brought these old assumptions into question and has thereby generated a wide variety of original, and often quite surprising, interpretations of the classics, as well as of rediscovered novels such as Kate Chopin's *The Awakening*, which has only recently entered the canon of works that scholars and critics study and that teachers assign their students.

The aim of The American Novel Series is to provide students of American literature and culture with introductory critical guides to

American novels now widely read and studied. Each volume is devoted to a single novel and begins with an introduction by the volume editor, a distinguished authority on the text. The introduction presents details of the novel's composition, publication, history, and contemporary reception, as well as a survey of the major critical trends and readings from first publication to the present. This overview is followed by four or five original essays, specifically commissioned from senior scholars of established reputation and from outstanding younger critics. Each essay presents a distinct point of view, and together they constitute a forum of interpretative methods and of the best contemporary ideas on each text.

It is our hope that these volumes will convey the vitality of current critical work in American literature, generate new insights and excitement for students of the American novel, and inspire new respects for and new perspectives upon these major literary texts.

Emory Elliott
University of California, Riverside

1

Introduction

MICHAEL AWKWARD

IN *Dust Tracks on a Road*, an autobiography written at the urging of her editor, Bertram Lippincott, Zora Neale Hurston expresses some dissatisfaction with her second novel, *Their Eyes Were Watching God*, which was published in 1937. She says of the novel:

> I wrote "Their Eyes Were Watching God" in Haiti. It was dammed up in me, and I wrote it under internal pressure in seven weeks. I wish that I could write it again. In fact, I regret all of my books. It is one of the tragedies of life that one cannot have all the wisdom one is ever to possess in the beginning. Perhaps, it is just as well to be rash and foolish for a while. If writers were too wise, perhaps no books would be written at all. It might be better to ask yourself "Why?" afterwards than before.[1]

Hurston voices the frustrations of an artist brought up in an oral culture like that of her birthplace, Eatonville, Florida, a source of inspiration throughout her writing career and, as she informs us on her autobiography's first page, the first black community in America "to be incorporated, the first attempt at organized self-government on the part of Negroes in America." In Eatonville, as Hurston writes in *Their Eyes Were Watching God*, storytellers sat on the porch of Mayor Joe Clarke's (Starks's in the novel) store and "passed around pictures of their thoughts for the others to look at and see" (48). Whereas these storytellers were able to retell, modify, and perfect the tales with which they entertained and enlightened other members of the community, authors such as Hurston had to be content with the successes they managed to achieve in written work which, with the seeming clarity of hindsight, might appear incomplete and hastily composed. Clearly, this is how she felt retrospectively about *Their Eyes Were Watching*

God, a work written to capture "all the tenderness of my passion" (and, it seems, at least some of her ambivalence about the physical and psychological violence) experienced during the relationship that inspired the novel.[2]

Her statement reflects some of the difficulties that Hurston experienced in navigating between two distinct narrative traditions – a black oral tradition characterized by active interchange between responsive storytellers and participatory listeners, and a (written) Western literary tradition where, typically, the author composes and the reader reads in isolation from the author – and suggests her interest in infusing the American novel with expressive potentialities derived from Afro-American culture. This statement and the narrative of *Their Eyes Were Watching God,* framed by a conversation wherein the protagonist, Janie, presents herself as a storyteller who will provide her audience – her best friend, Pheoby – "de understandin' " (7) of her life story, suggest Hurston's experimental impulse, her desire to employ the novel form as a means to preserve and transmit Afro-American oral narrative practices. In the frame of her novel, Hurston approximates the relationship between speaker and listener in Afro-American expressivity, offering in *Their Eyes Were Watching God* what Henry Louis Gates, Jr., has called a "speakerly text."[3]

Hurston's autobiographical comments also read as a prophetic warning against the types of "rash and foolish" judgments about her life and work that have led to a devaluation of her accomplishments. Her novel was not widely recognized as an important achievement until long after an impoverished Hurston, seriously ill after suffering a stroke in 1959, died of heart disease in 1960 without funds to provide for a proper burial. In fact, although the novel did receive a few positive reviews from critics – for example, Sterling Brown wrote in a review for *The Nation* that the novel "is chock-full of earthy and touching poetry" – the initial impression of *Their Eyes Were Watching God* in Afro-American literary circles was that it was a seriously flawed text. Such a view was expressed by Alain Locke in the journal *Opportunity.* Despite his belief that Hurston was a "talented writer" with a "gift for poetic phrase, for rare dialect and folk humor," Locke, an enthusiastic earlier supporter of Hurston's work and her teacher at Howard University, viewed the novel as an "over-simplification" of the Afro-American situation in the post-Reconstruction South, and felt Hurston had not "come to grips with motive fiction and social document fiction." Even more harsh than Locke in his appraisal was Richard Wright, the most widely read and celebrated black American writer during the last two decades of Hurston's life. Wright saw *Their Eyes Were Watching God* as lacking material that lent itself to "significant interpretation." Further, Wright argued, in a review that appeared in *New Masses*, that the novel evidences Hurston's shameless pandering

> to a white audience whose chauvinistic tastes she knows how to satisfy. She exploits that phase of Negro life which is "quaint," the phase which evokes a piteous smile on the lips of the "superior" race.[4]

Such negative reactions were to become quite common, and made an unbiased evaluation of Hurston's work nearly impossible during her lifetime. Locke's and Wright's responses seem largely to have been inspired by two perceptions that were to persist, virtually unquestioned, until recently: (1) that the black artist's primary responsibility was to create protest fiction that explored America's historical mistreatment of blacks, boosting black self-esteem and changing racist white attitudes about Afro-Americans in the process; and (2) that in both her public life and her work, Hurston was, to use poet Langston Hughes's phrase, "a perfect 'darkie,' in the nice meaning [whites] give the term – that is a naive, childlike, sweet, humorous, and highly colored Negro."[5] Nothing that Hurston ever wrote convinced her contemporaries of the limitations either of didactic polemical fiction or of derisive biographical criticism of her work. And none of her defenders during her lifetime was able to read these limitations as persuasively as contemporary scholars such as Barbara Johnson, who has asserted:

> While Hurston has often been read and judged on the basis of personality alone, her "racy" adoption of "happy darkie" stance, which was a successful strategy for survival, does not by any means exhaust the representational strategies of her writing.[6]

3

Johnson's statement suggests the fruitfulness for contemporary readers of looking past the numerous attacks on Hurston's character and closely examining the works of this prolific and provocative Afro-American woman writer. Indeed, the critical standing of few novels in American literary history has profited more from a second look than has *Their Eyes Were Watching God*. After years of general neglect, *Their Eyes Were Watching God* has since the early 1980s achieved a position of prominence within the American literary tradition. Hurston's second novel, written in 1936 during a folklore-gathering expedition in Haiti while the author was recovering from a painful relationship with a younger man (a relationship that served in essential ways as emotional fodder for her novel), has come to be widely considered one of the important American novels produced during this century. The novel has become a commercial success as well: Although it sold poorly during her lifetime, in just over ten years since its reissue by the University of Illinois Press – a reissue no doubt encouraged by the success of that press's 1977 publication of Robert Hemenway's highly acclaimed literary biography of Hurston – *Their Eyes Were Watching God* has sold well over 200,000 copies.[7]

Clearly, conditions have developed to cause what Arna Bontemps, before the current Hurston boom, spoke of as that "tiny shift of gravity [that] could have made them [Hurston's works] best-sellers."[8] Proof of this shift can be found in the numbers of scholars specializing in emergent or well-established critical traditions who have chosen recently to place Hurston's novel at the center of their canons. For example, male Afro-Americanist literary critics,[9] white feminist critics,[10] and mainstream canonical critics[11] have begun to discuss in illuminating ways the significance of Hurston's work.

Further, many black feminist scholars view *Their Eyes Were Watching God* as "a forerunner of the [Afro-American women's] fiction of the seventies and eighties,"[12] and believe that "[s]everal black women writers, among them some of the most accomplished in America today, are repeating, imitating, or revising her narrative strategies. . . . Alice Walker, Toni Morrison, Toni Cade Bambara, Gloria Naylor and Jamaica Kincaid, among others, seem to have grounded their fictions in the works of Zora Neale

Hurston. . . . They are a tradition within the tradition – voices that are black and women's."[13]

Public utterances about Hurston by contemporary Afro-American women novelists suggest the accuracy of this last statement. Indeed, the author of the prize-winning novel *The Color Purple,* Alice Walker, has been the single most instrumental figure in the recent establishment of Hurston's literary reputation. Walker published several provocative essays during the 1970s which brought Hurston's work to the attention of many, and said of *Their Eyes Were Watching God,* "There is no book more important to me than this one." Walker also paid her debt to Hurston by locating and marking her previously unmarked grave with a tombstone designating her literary forebear as "A Genius of the South."[14] Other writers have more recently acknowledged the impact of Hurston's work on their own. For example, Gloria Naylor, author of *The Women of Brewster Place,* has asserted that Hurston's vivid description of a hurricane's destructive force in *Their Eyes Were Watching God* contributed to her own delineation of a hurricane in her latest novel, *Mama Day.*[15]

If Hurston is indeed correct in her assertion that "[i]t might be better to ask yourself 'Why?' afterwards than before," one question we might profitably ask is why her novel was neglected for so long. Why was *Their Eyes Were Watching God,* a work now viewed by a multitude of readers as remarkably successful in its complex, satisfyingly realized depiction of its Afro-American female protagonist's search for self and community, ever relegated to the margins of the canon? Before we can begin to answer this crucial question, we must first acknowledge several essential facts about the novel's initial and contemporary reception. First of all – unlike, for example, Harriet Wilson's recently discovered 1859 novel, *Our Nig* – *Their Eyes Were Watching God* was not totally ignored by book reviewers upon its publication. In fact, it received a certain amount of attention, albeit cursory and largely misinformed, both from important figures within Afro-American literary circles like Wright and Locke, and from white book reviewers working for prominent periodicals like the *Saturday Review* and the *New York Post,* some of whom appeared to have liked Hurston's novel much more than did her Afro-American contemporaries. One such reviewer, George Stevens, wrote in the *Saturday Review of Literature* that except for some weaknesses in execution, "the narration is exactly right, because most of it is in dialogue, and the dialogue gives us a constant sense of character in action. No one has ever reported the speech of Negroes with a more accurate ear for its raciness." He ended his review by calling *Their Eyes Were Watching God* a "simple and unpretentious story, but there is nothing else quite like it." Another reviewer, Hershel Brickell of the *New York Post*, favorably compared Hurston's ability to render sensory experience to that of D. H. Lawrence.[16]

Hurston was by no means an obscure or unknown writer. As Hemenway explains, "She had been granted honorary doctorates, published in national magazines, featured on the cover of the *Saturday Review*, invited to speak at major universities, and praised by the *New York Herald Tribune* as being 'in the front rank' not only of black writers but of all American writers."[17] And although *Their Eyes Were Watching God* did not receive the acclaim that greeted, for example, Wright's *Native Son* three years later, it did, nonetheless, receive a certain amount of attention from major publications, and several positive reviews. Despite this recognition, Hurston's novel quickly disappeared from the minds of readers and critics, selling fewer than 5,000 copies before going out of print.[18]

Also, we need to recognize that, if *Their Eyes Were Watching God* was not widely read until the late 1970s, critics did, as early as the 1950s, sing its praises and argue for its central position in the American literary tradition. For example, Robert Bone offered in 1958 what appears to be the first glowing praise of Hurston's novel by an influential American literary scholar. Bone called it "Miss Hurston's best novel, and possibly the best novel of the period, excepting *Native Son*."[19] After the 1960s, a decade in which Hurston's contributions were generally ignored (an exception is Julius Lester's dedication of his book *Black Folktales* to the "memory of Zora Neale Hurston, who made me glad I am me"), the early 1970s witnessed a sharp increase in statements by critics frustrated by the continued marginality of *Their Eyes Were Watching God*. For example, June Jordan characterized Hurston's second novel as "the prototypical Black novel of affirmation" and as "the most successful, convincing, and exemplary novel of Blacklove that we have." Larry Neal, who saw in it evidence that Hurston possessed "a rather remarkable understanding of a blues aesthetic and its accompanying sensibility," considered *Their Eyes Were Watching God* "clearly her best novel." In addition, Roger Whitlow called the novel "one of the fine works of American literature of this century," and Addison Gayle called it "a novel of intense power . . . [that] evidences the strength and promise of African-American culture."[20]

These and other discussions kept alive an awareness of Hurston's novel until a time when members of the literary academy were more able to appreciate *Their Eyes Were Watching God*. Such a time was signaled by two significant changes that occurred in the 1970s: the establishment of feminist literary criticism within the academy as an important interpretative strategy, and the emergence of culturally specific forms of evaluation of Afro-American texts grounded in the black American oral storytelling traditions and discursive practices, or what I call throughout this introduction "Afrocentric criticism."

Indeed, Henry Louis Gates is correct in his suggestion that the efforts of his generation of black and feminist critics have established Hurston as an important part of the canon of American literature.[21] The emergence of feminist criticism was crucial because it brought new attention to neglected works by women authors such as Hurston, and developed interpretative practices adequate to the explication of these works. The burgeoning of Afrocentric strategies of analysis was equally important to the rediscovery of *Their Eyes Were Watching God*, for such strategies provided readers with the capacity to respond to elements crucial to a comprehension of Hurston's artistic sensibilities.

The previous obscurity of Hurston's novel was not the result of benign neglect. Rather, it was a product both of the difficulty that Afro-American and female writers generally encountered in having their work taken seriously by critics, and of Hurston's aesthetic and ideological differences with other members of the literary community about the function of art and the depiction of Afro-Americans in literature. And contemporary acclaim for Hurston's novel results from the emergence to prominence of literary critics whose ideological perspectives and assumptions about aesthetics allowed them to appreciate *Their Eyes Were Watching God*. Such a statement should in no way detract from the reader's sense of the novel's power or its contemporary standing. Acknowledging the ties between Hurston's current importance and the belief systems of members of the literary academy allows us to explore the conditions that have allowed Hurston to assume a central position in the American literary canon.

The emergence of previously unvalued works like *Their Eyes Were Watching God* or, for that matter, Kate Chopin's *The Awakening*, along with a clear-sighted examination of literary history and the sharply fluctuating reputations of many important American novelists, insists that we view a literary text's achievement of canonicity, its accomplishment of a (perhaps temporary) place of significance in the academy and the culture, as "radically contingent." Barbara Herrnstein Smith uses this phrase to indicate her belief that the value of a literary work is "neither fixed, an inherent quality, or an objective property of things, but, rather, an effect of multiple, continuously changing, and continuously interacting variables."[22]

We can test the validity of Smith's assertions concerning the "contingency of value" by exploring briefly the example of Ernest Hemingway, whose reputation has suffered greatly since the 1970s. In many critical circles, the qualities for which his work previously had been valued – its cryptic style, its advocacy of reticence, machismo, and grace under the pressures of what has been conceived by many intellectuals as a godless, chaotic modern world – are seen either to have been thoroughly absorbed into our culture (e.g., Hemingway's dedication to the expurgation of wordiness and sentimentality which, in his estimation, had formerly characterized much of American fiction) or, as in the case of his "code," to have been called into question or generally devalued. As a consequence, critics who wish to maintain for the novelist a prominent position within the American canon have begun to set forth a version of Hemingway radically distinct from the hypermasculine personality that occupied the attention of his earlier admirers. This "new" Hemingway is, as one critic recently has claimed, a male feminist par excellence, a writer acutely attuned to

8

the socially constructed nature of gender and to the difficulties of women's position within patriarchical society:

> [T]he influence of feminist criticism seems to have been most in-
> strumental in reviving interest in Hemingway's life and work. For
> his macho posturing and the insipidity of some of his heroines he
> was the man feminists loved to hate when they began in the early
> 1970s to resurvey the cultural meaning of American literature. But
> this criticism ultimately also led to a fresh examination of his fiction
> and to the discovery in some of it of a heretofore neglected strain,
> one which was unusually alert to female sensibilities.[23]

My interest here is not to discuss which version of Hemingway is more consistent with the texts the writer produced, but, rather, in order to examine the emergence of *Their Eyes Were Watching God,* to point out the degree to which our perceptions of the meaning and importance of a text are affected by variables other than what we once believed to be pure artistic value untied to any ideologically informed conditions. If the words on the pages of *A Farewell to Arms* and *Their Eyes Were Watching God* are visibly unchanged from one edition of the texts to the next, surely their critics and readers have indeed changed. Barbara Herrnstein Smith offers an insightful analysis of literary value that aids in our comprehension of the emergence of a feminist Hemingway and, more essential for our purposes here, the recent canonization of *Their Eyes Were Watching God.* In an exploration of the conditions that motivate the emergence or reemergence of works of art, Smith argues that a text

> may . . . be subsequently "rediscovered" as an "unjustly neglected
> masterpiece," either when the functions it had originally performed
> are again desired/able or, what is more likely, when different of its
> properties and possible functions become foregrounded by a new
> set of subjects with emergent interests and purposes.[24]

If Smith's formulations are correct, then we must understand that both the rediscovery of *Their Eyes Were Watching God* and its earlier obscurity result from the perceptions of the novel's utility and the degree to which it can be seen as meeting "emergent interests and purposes." We can comprehend the initial obscurity of Hurston's novel, particularly its failure to achieve prominence within American literature of a kind with the works of such contemporaries of Hurston as Wright and Langston Hughes, in the context of debates within Afro-American literary circles during the first half of the twentieth century concerning the propagandistic utility of black literary texts. In an era when Afro-American literature was viewed by many black intellectuals and white readers as an occasion for direct confrontation of white America's racist practices and its effects on Afro-Americans, Hurston's imaginative landscape, which generally did not include maniacal white villains or, for that matter, superhumanly proud, long suffering blacks, seemed inappropriate and hopelessly out of step. In addition to the gender-determined nature of literary reputations during the period, when it was generally the case among Afro-Americans that only male writers were provided with the types of emotional and financial nurturance and publishing contacts necessary to sustain a literary career, Hurston's reputation also suffered as a consequence of disputes about how blacks ought to be portrayed in literature. Sensitive to the need to improve white America's perception of Afro-Americans, some powerful black intellectuals, including Locke and W. E. B. Du Bois, believing that literature represented the most effective means by which to begin to dispel racist notions that black Americans were morally and cognitively subhuman, insisted that Afro-American writers were obligated to present Afro-Americans in the most favorable – and flattering – light possible.

Encouraging a literature that took as its primary subject the Afro-American middle class, a then-small segment of the black population whose sensibilities were most closely aligned with those of a white middle-class readership, these intellectuals were often openly hostile to the texts of writers like Langston Hughes, the Jamaican-born poet and novelist Claude McKay, and Hurston. The work of these figures emphasized the Afro-American masses, working- and lower-class rural Southerners (Hurston's special interest), and urban Northerners (Hughes's primary focus) whose lives suggested that they had resisted what Hughes called the "urge within the [black] race toward whiteness, the desire to pour racial individuality into the mold of American standardization, and to be as little Negro and as much American as possible."[25] These writers recognized the poetry of the black folk preacher's

10

sermon, the sophisticated sensibilities found in the blues and in jazz, and the musicality and figurative complexity of black vernacular speech, at a time when a large number of Afro-Americans urged that these expressive forms be abandoned because they were markers of difference and persistent, shameful vestiges of black enslavement on American shores.

To put the matter more succinctly, Afro-American intellectuals were involved in a battle over whether to emphasize likeness or difference, Americanness or blackness. This was a battle which, coupled with the added burden of her gender that rendered Hurston marginal to begin with, made full appreciation of her talents virtually impossible during the first half of the twentieth century. If we are now able to recognize in Hurston's work similarities with that of a more immediately embraced Langston Hughes or a much praised Jean Toomer in its experiential thrust and its employment of and respect for Afro-American expressive traditions, we must acknowledge that the male intellectuals who appreciated Hughes's and Toomer's experimentations did not closely explore Hurston's texts in large part because of her gender. The sophisticated themes of Hurston's work were not seriously considered by readers unprepared for her subtle delineations of Afro-American lives or for her often female centered concerns, both of which are fully evident in *Their Eyes Were Watching God*. Surveying some of the early responses to the novel provides us with invaluable insight into the assumptions and interpretative agendas of its readers which blinded them to the strengths of Hurston's novel.

A particularly fruitful way to begin such an examination is by taking a closer look at Richard Wright's aforementioned review. Wright's response focuses on what he believes is absent from *Their Eyes Were Watching God*. He argues that Hurston's novel fails to possess

> a basic idea or theme that lends itself to significant interpreta-
> tion. . . . [Hurston's] dialogue manages to catch the psychological
> movements of the Negro folk-mind in their pure simplicity, but
> that's as far as it goes. . . . The sensory sweep of her novel carries *no
> theme, no message, no thought*.[26]

What Wright purports to be absent from *Their Eyes Were Watching God* — "theme," "message," "thought" — is a function not of the

11

novel's deficiencies, but, rather, of its own interpretative blindness, of what Wright himself cannot see.[27] If one is attentive, for example, to the theme of patriarchal power as it is delineated in *Their Eyes Were Watching God* – an issue which contemporary readers are much better equipped to deal with than were readers when Wright's review appeared, and one which dominated the late 1970s and early 1980s responses to Hurston's novel – quickly it becomes clear that the text does indeed "lend . . . itself to significant interpretation."

That Wright was unable to recognize this thematic element resulted from his inability to observe the feminist impulses operative in Hurston's novel (or, to put the matter another way, his inability to see them *as significant*) and, further, from his vision of Afro-American literature. Wright saw black expressive art as a blunt weapon to be used to expose the effects upon Euro-Americans and Afro-Americans of what he was later to term the white "force" of American racism. Hurston's work emphasized her belief that perspectives other than Wright's stark social realism were possible for Afro-American literature and necessary for its growth; further, it demonstrated a faith in Afro-American people and in the strength of their culture and its belief systems which Wright's work seems clearly to lack. Wright's view of literature, along with his apparent lack of interest in the significance of female oppression within American capitalism, rendered him unable to appreciate Hurston's subtle critiques of such elements in American society as materialism, sexism, racism, and classism.

While Wright's is certainly among the most hostile early responses to *Their Eyes Were Watching God*, it shares with other reactions to Hurston limitations that inhibit an appreciation of the novel's significant contribution to the delineation of the particular difficulties encountered by black women within racist and sexist social institutions. For example, despite its author's clearly more favorable perception of Hurston's literary gifts, Carl Milton Hughes's comments about *Their Eyes Were Watching God* reflect, like Wright's, a peculiarly gendered bias and blindness. Although Hughes praises Hurston as "an author of long standing and high attainment [who] manifests interest in varied activities and manages to accomplish a great deal in all," his discussion of *Their Eyes*

Were Watching God suggests that he had not read the novel closely, and that his appreciation of it was narrow indeed. Hughes says of Hurston's second novel:

> In *Their Eyes Were Watching God*, she made a significant contribution to the field of American literature, using Negro themes. Her character, Teacake [*sic*], introduced to literature a particular type which remains unique. . . . Even though the cause of Teacake's [*sic*] madness could be attributed to snake bite, the force with which this madness comes to the reader makes Teacake [*sic*] a memorable character.[28] (172)

There are obvious factual errors here; we know, of course, that Tea Cake's madness results not from snake venom, but, rather, from being bitten by a rabid dog. But more problematic than Hughes's inability to recall the origins of the male character's malady is his insistence that it is Tea Cake, and not Janie (whose story it is the stated purpose of *Their Eyes Were Watching God* to articulate), who represents that which is "unique" and "memorable" in Hurston's novel. For a mind, like Hughes's, "steeped in maleness,"[29] Hurston's delineation of Tea Cake is generally more provocative and expertly wrought than the author's extended figuration of the female protagonist's attempts to achieve a sense of self in a variety of Florida communities in which black women are viewed as men's pliable possessions. In Hughes's emphasis on Tea Cake and his descent into madness, both Janie and the novel's profound critique of the institution of marriage and of other institutions that appear to naturalize male superiority are effectively erased from Hurston's story. (Hughes does not even mention Janie in his overview of the novel!)

Carl Hughes's response is suggestive of the types of erasures and misrepresentations to which Hurston's life and texts were subjected following her appearance in New York in 1925 as a flamboyant, talented, oratorically gifted participant in the Harlem Renaissance. In fact, until recently, it was primarily through often malicious (mis)representations of her, through the stories that were told of her by her male contemporaries and literary historians, that Hurston was known to us.

One of the most frequently cited depictions of Hurston appears in Langston Hughes's autobiography, *The Big Sea*. Long considered the most important Afro-American writer to have emerged from the Harlem Renaissance, Hughes (no relation to Carl Hughes) produced what was the movement's de facto manifesto. In a 1926 essay entitled "The Negro Artist and the Racial Mountain," Hughes urged black artists to reject the condescending and shame-filled Afro-American middle-class attitudes about black folk art such as jazz, the blues, and gospels, and insisted on a revised Afro-American aesthetic that presented the Afro-American masses – and black folk cultural products – at the center of the black writer's interests. Hughes argued that the Afro-American "low-down folks, the so-called common element . . . furnish a wealth of colorful, distinctive material for any artist because they still hold their own individuality in the face of American standardization." In many respects – particularly as evidenced in their works' focus on the Afro-American masses and their infusion of traditional Western literary genres with the discursive and formal properties of Afro-American folk forms – Hughes and Hurston possessed kindred artistic spirits. And for a brief period, these writers were close friends and artistic collaborators. This relationship ended, however, with a bitter dispute between Hurston and Hughes over control of a play they coauthored entitled "Mule Bone."[30]

Despite their artistic commonalities, Hughes's description of Hurston concentrates not on her literary texts, but, rather, on Hurston *as text:*

> Of this [the Harlem Renaissance] "niggerati," Zora Neale Hurston was certainly the most amusing. Only to reach a wider audience, need she ever write books – because *she is a perfect book of entertainment in herself.* In her youth she was always getting scholarships and things from wealthy white people, some of whom simply paid her just to sit around and represent the Negro race for them, and she did it in such a racy fashion. She was full of side-splitting anecdotes, humorous tales, and tragicomic stories, remembered out of her life in the south as a daughter of a travelling minister of God. She could make you laugh one minute and cry the next. To many of her white friends, no doubt, she was a perfect "darkie," in the nice meaning they give the term – that is a naive, childlike, sweet, humorous, and highly colored Negro.[31]

Hughes fails here to take Hurston seriously as a writer. Whereas, in an otherwise informative description of the Harlem Renaissance

14

and its important literary figures, Hughes discusses males such as Jean Toomer, Countee Cullen, and Rudolph Fisher as *authors*, as writers with serious literary talents in whose works he is thoughtfully engaged, he fails even to mention a single text that comprised Hurston's literary output during or after the Renaissance. Thus, whereas the novelist Wallace Thurman's works are termed "important," "compelling" and "superb," Hurston is figured as a character, as "a perfect book of entertainment in herself" who "[o]nly to reach a wider audience, need . . . ever write books."

For Hughes, Hurston was not an effective creative artist, not a serious writer, but a figure whose most notable talent was her ability to present the materials of others in dramatic fashion. She was, in Hughes's view, merely a vessel for the articulation of extant Afro-American texts and cultural forms, not an artist capable of transforming folk material remembered from her Eatonville childhood or gathered during anthropological expeditions and making it her own. Whether he is motivated here simply by an androcentrism that cannot accommodate a vision of black women as serious writers or, more likely, by a continued bitterness toward Hurston arising from their legal squabbles, it is clear that Hughes fails to view Hurston as an imaginative *writer.*

Hughes's perception of Hurston was quite influential, and, along with other such discussions of her career, helped to shape impressions of her through the early 1970s.[32] Hurston's position within American letters began to change only when critics, impressed by her work and particularly by *Their Eyes Were Watching God,* explored the interpretative assumptions that precipitated and served to perpetuate her continuing marginal status. For example, June Jordan argued that Hurston's obscurity was a product of "white, mass-media manipulation" which celebrates only one black writer at a time, and which has popularized among Afro-Americans the "notion that only one kind of writing – protest writing . . . deserves our support and study" (4, 5). For Jordan, a work like *Their Eyes Were Watching God,* an "affirmation of Black values and life-style within the American context,"[33] was doomed to obscurity by the popularity of Richard Wright, whose texts projected a significantly more hostile and antagonistic attitude toward white American racism. Jordan calls for a rejection of interpretative politics that insist that we privilege one writer's approach to the delineation of the Afro-American situation over the other. Alice Walker, on the other hand, in response to "the misleading, deliberatedly belittling, inaccurate, and generally irresponsible attacks on her work and life,"[34] suggests that Hurston's marginality resulted from a general devaluation of her informed and vigorous delineations of black southern folk culture, and disapproval of her refusal to submit to extant expectations for Afro-American women's comportment. She was, in Walker's view, a shocking presence for Northerners only nominally interested in authentic black folk culture, a truly Afrocentric woman writer whose perspectives on marriage, Africa, acceptable behavior for black women, and the uses of folklore in Afro-American literature were well ahead of her time.

Such responses were followed by a diverse body of thoughtful and provocative scholarship on *Their Eyes Were Watching God*. Robert Hemenway's *Zora Neale Hurston: A Literary Biography* and the re-publication of *Their Eyes Were Watching God*, both by the University of Illinois Press, and the Feminist Press's collection of Hurston's writings, *I Love Myself When I Am Laughing*, edited by Walker, helped to establish the novel as a presence in the marketplace and as an important rediscovery whose contours needed to be explored. Critics have successfully taken up the challenge of explicating Hurston's novel. This criticism has focused primarily on two areas of concern: (1) the nature and meaning of Hurston's delineations of Janie's responses to patriarchal attempts to limit her to circumscribed, unfulfilling roles; and (2) Hurston's use in the narrative of black vernacular discourse and Afro-American storytelling conventions.

The former area has concerned readers interested in the degree to which Janie's movement toward self-actualization, her response to patriarchal power, is successful. A useful example of this approach is Lloyd Brown's essay, "Zora Neale Hurston and the Nature of Female Perception." Brown examines what he calls Hurston's "best novel" by reading its action against its two opening paragraphs where Hurston offers "a rather bold claim about the perceptual differences between men and women." For Brown, these paragraphs provide the novelist's view that "it is a male characteristic to accept the thwarting of dreams with resignation"

16

and "what Hurston clearly regards as a peculiarly female transcendentalism ('women forget all those things they don't want to remember. . . . The dream is the truth')." Brown notes striking similarities between Hurston's representation of the nature of female perception and Simone de Beauvoir's assertion that it "is a female trait . . . to use dreams as a means of transcending rather than resigning to reality: dreams are the woman's means of compensating for a sense of subordination (immanence) through the 'realm of imagination.' "[35]

Brown not only suggests the sophistication of Hurston's thought (i.e., by comparing her formulations to those of one of the century's most respected feminist thinkers), but he also provides readers with a means of responding to troubling elements of *Their Eyes Were Watching God*. To assert, as other essays have done, that the novel is essentially a story of Janie's achievement of self made possible, in part, by her relationship with Tea Cake, one needs also to make sense of evidence in the text that Janie's third husband is a less than ideal mate. His positive contributions to Janie's life are significant, but Tea Cake also steals from Janie, encourages the advances of another woman, strikes his wife in an attempt to ward off a potential rival for Janie's affections, and exhibits other evidence of traditional sexist male attitudes concerning women. Instead of viewing Tea Cake as the personification of Janie's dream in her grandmother's backyard of an ideal mate, Brown notes that Janie is able to think of him as such because her highly developed imagination allows her, after her self-defensive murder of a rabid Tea Cake, to forget her third husband's baleful behavior and remember only what she loves and cherishes in him. The text is clear in its insistence that Tea Cake has internalized much of his culture's belief about masculine and feminine roles.

Tea Cake is described in quite impressive terms, including in the following passage which provides an outstanding example of Hurston's masterful and frequently moving prose:

> She couldn't make him look just like any other man to her. He could be a bee to a blossom — a pear tree blossom in the spring. He seemed to be crushing scent out of the world with his footsteps. Crushing aromatic herbs with every step he took. Spices hung about him.He was a glance from God. (101–2)

This passage contains telling qualifications of Janie's impressions of Tea Cake – introduced by the narrator ("could be," "seemed") – which locate these perceptions firmly within the mind of a hesitant but lovestruck Janie who, after two unfulfilling marriages, has kept alive inside herself the image of an ideal, essentially flawless mate which she initially conceives during her sexual awakening in Nanny's backyard. The beauty of Hurston's language mirrors the seductiveness of Janie's dream, elevating a generally likeable Tea Cake to a status no realistically delineated figure could maintain. That he is not able to achieve such an exalted status is not surprising. What is surprising, what makes her complex delineation of Janie and Tea Cake's relationship especially provocative, is Hurston's concern with the potentially debilitating consequences for both males and females of placing their mates on pedestals whose foundations are shaky at best.

Brown's essay is a representative of an important, female-centered element in the responses to the novel published since the 1980s. The other most compelling approach focuses on the nature of Hurston's employment of black vernacular discourse and story-telling practices in *Their Eyes Were Watching God*. In several respects, these critical concerns cannot be easily separated from each other, for a major feature of Janie's plight is the fact that she is denied access to the expressive rituals and traditions of the Eatonville community because of her gender. In fact, Robert Hemenway has argued that *Their Eyes Were Watching God* is a record of Hurston's discovery of "one of the flaws in her early memories of the village [of Eatonville]: there had usually been only men telling lies on the front porch of Joe Clarke's store."[36] Janie's is a struggle for voice, for the ability to display her grasp of the sophisticated tropes of black vernacular expressivity in order to be able to participate in the storytelling sessions that took place in Eatonville and that helped to determine one's status within the community. Further, Janie seeks to demonstrate to Joe Starks, who silences her repeatedly throughout their marriage, the quality of her thought. In short, Janie's achievement of verbal power may allow her to become a fully active agent both within the community and within her marriage.

18

The critical emphasis on Hurston's employment of black expressive traditions has, somewhat ironically, led to charges that Hurston's narrative strategies are unsound. Robert Stepto has offered the most cogent and influential statement concerning what he calls the "one great flaw" in *Their Eyes Were Watching God*. He argues that

> Hurston creates the essential illusion that Janie has achieved her voice. . . . But the tale undercuts much of this, not because of its content . . . but because of its narration. Hurston's curious insistence on having Janie's tale . . . told by an omnisc[i]ent third person, rather than a first-person narrator, implies that Janie has not really won her voice and self after all.[37]

Other critics, including Bernard Bell and Lillie Howard, although less skeptical than Stepto about Janie's accomplishments, have similar reservations about Hurston's failure to allow Janie to tell her own story within the pages of *Their Eyes Were Watching God* and, thus, demonstrate her achievement of expressive power.[38]

The most effective responses to such readings have attempted to explain Hurston's narrative choices in terms of her innovative employment of Afro-American expressive paradigms and practices. For example, John Callahan, after noting the initial persuasiveness of Stepto's perspectives on his own thinking, argues that

> Hurston, always eclectic, original, idiosyncratic, individual, experimental, had decided to challenge the once innovative and generative but by the mid-1930s increasingly pat and closed modernist position against fraternization between novelist and character. . . . In *Their Eyes Were Watching God* Hurston breathes into her third-person narration the living voice of a storyteller. Implicitly, she puts her personality on the line. For the fashionable value of authorial control she substitutes a rhetoric of intimacy developed from the collaborative habit of call-and-response. . . . Because of her intimate yet impersonal form, Hurston invites her readers to respond as listeners and participants in the work of storytelling.[39]

Although Callahan's response certainly does not settle this debate, it persuasively indicates that the success of the narrative strategies of *Their Eyes Were Watching God* needs to be measured not against modernist conventions which fuel the work of Euro-American writers, but, rather, in terms of the quality of her incorporations of black expressive principles into the genre of the novel. Callahan conceives of Hurston's narrative as an inventive employment of the black verbal behavior call-and-response which encourages participatory reading. Readings such as Callahan's argue that Hurston's narrative strategies produce in *Their Eyes Were Watching God* an empowering work that gives voice to the voiceless both in her narrative and outside of it, including Afro-American women whose situation within racist and sexist cultural systems had never before (and has rarely since) been so compellingly delineated.

The following essays offer provocative new thoughts on *Their Eyes Were Watching God*. Written by literary scholars who have all commented on Hurston's work elsewhere,[40] these essays respond to issues that have characterized the critical discourse surrounding *Their Eyes Were Watching God* and represent profitable areas of future analysis. Exploring what he terms "the personal dimension" in *Their Eyes Were Watching God*, Robert Hemenway disputes claims concerning Hurston's relationships with white patrons which insist that "she was more comfortable under these arrangements than many of her Negro contemporaries,"[41] and argues that her novel sheds light on her "struggle to dramatize folklore as a sign of cultural difference." Nellie McKay reads *Their Eyes Were Watching God* as an autobiographical form in which Janie speaks herself into being with and through the voice of the omniscient narrator, and one where Hurston offers what is, in effect, the text of the liberation of her own authorial voice. Also interested in the ways in which the novel reflects Hurston's dilemmas as a writer, Hazel Carby considers the reasons for Hurston's focus in her second novel and elsewhere on the town of Eatonville (especially considering the widespread Afro-American migration from the rural South to urban centers in the North), and discerns in *Their Eyes Were Watching God* Hurston's self-conscious romanticization of black Southern rural life which reflects her recognition – like Janie's upon her return to Eatonville – of the inherent difficulties for the black artist in a return to the folk. And Rachel Blau DuPlessis employs a feminist interpretative strategy that foregrounds, in her words, "the interplay of as many social determinants as can

be . . . seen in the text — in narrative choices, structures, outcomes, . . . and in the web of circumstances surrounding [it], . . .
especially its fabrication and reception," to explore many elements
of Hurston's novel, including its trial scenes and its title which,
though considered "magical" by Alain Locke and other readers,[42]
has not been seriously considered heretofore.

Taken together, these essays reflect the faith of the contributors
that *Their Eyes Were Watching God* possesses a power and insight
that should continue to compel, inspire, and fascinate readers of
American novels.

NOTES

1. Zora Neale Hurston, *Dust Tracks on a Road,* ed. Robert Hemenway
   (1942. Reprint: Urbana: University of Illinois Press, 1984), p. 212.
2. For Hurston's discussion of her relationship with the man she identifies only as A. W. P., see *Dust Tracks,* pp. 252–62. There are striking
   similarities, I feel, between Janie's marriages and Hurston's relationship with this figure whom she shrouds in mystery. One notes, for
   example, connections between Joe Starks's attempts to gain Janie's
   submission to his authority and A. W. P.'s efforts to transform Hurston
   into an obedient, submissive mate. Both of these efforts take the form
   of the male's attempt to deny to the female the power of voice: Starks
   commands an oratorically gifted Janie not to participate in the verbal
   rituals of the Eatonville community, and A. W. P. demands that
   Hurston abandon her burgeoning writing career. Hurston uses elements of this younger man's character in her depictions of both Joe
   Starks and Tea Cake, a fact which suggests that Janie's last two husbands share more in common than the criticism of *Their Eyes Were
   Watching God* has heretofore noted.
3. Henry Louis Gates, Jr., "Zora Neale Hurston and the Speakerly Text,"
   in *The Signifying Monkey: A Theory of Afro-American Literary Criticism*
   (New York: Oxford University Press, 1988), pp. 170–216. In one of
   the most illuminating discussions of the novel to date, Gates argues
   that "Hurston's narrative strategy seems to concern itself with the
   possibilities of representation of the speaking black voice in writing"
   (xxv). Although I will later have more to say about the question of the
   narrative strategies of *Their Eyes Were Watching God,* it is important to

note here that Gates seeks a means of accounting for Hurston's movement between standard English and black vernacular, and also her
motivation for her framing of the novel with a conversation between
Janie and Pheoby. As we shall see, these choices – especially the
frame of the novel – have provoked debate among Hurston's critics.
For a further discussion of the debate, see Michael Awkward, "'The
inaudible voice of it all': Silence, Voice, and Action in *Their Eyes Were
Watching God*," in *Inspiriting Influences: Tradition, Revision, and Afro-
American Women's Novels* (New York: Columbia University Press,
1989), pp. 15–56. Interesting discussions of the issue of creating
speakerly possibilities in written texts – a concern Hurston shares
with many Afro-American writers – are offered in Gates, *The Signify-
ing Monkey*; John Wideman, "The Black Writer and the Magic of the
Word," *New York Times Book Review* (January 24, 1988), 1, 28–9; Toni
Morrison, "Rootedness: The Ancestor as Foundation," in *Black Women
Writers (1950–1980)*, ed. Mari Evans (Garden City, NJ: Doubleday,
1984), pp. 339–45; John Callahan, *In the African-American Grain: The
Pursuit of Voice in Twentieth-Century Black Fiction* (Urbana: University of
Illinois Press, 1988); and Robert Stepto, "Distrust of the Reader in
Afro-American Narratives," in *Reconstructing American Literary History*,
ed. Sacvan Bercovitch (Cambridge, MA: Harvard University Press,
1986), pp. 300–22.

4. Sterling Brown, "Luck Is a Fortune," *The Nation* 166 (October 16,
1937): 409–10; Alain Locke, "Jingo, Counter-Jingo, and Us," *Opportunity* 16 (January 1938): 10; and Richard Wright, "Between Laughter and Tears," *New Masses* 25 (October 5, 1937): 22–5.

5. Langston Hughes, *The Big Sea* (New York: Hill and Wang, 1940), p.
239. I will discuss Hughes's perceptions of Hurston more fully later in
the Introduction.

6. Barbara Johnson, "Thresholds of Difference: Structures of Address in
Zora Neale Hurston," *A World of Difference*, (Baltimore: Johns Hopkins
University Press, 1987), pp. 173–4.

7. The *New York Times Book Review* 92 (October 11, 1987): 58, lists the
number of University of Illinois sales at 240,000. In "The Master's
Pieces: On Canon Formation and the Afro-American Tradition," a
lecture delivered at the University of Michigan, January 24, 1989, as
part of the series "New Words, New Thoughts: Rereading Zora Neale
Hurston's *Their Eyes Were Watching God*," Henry Louis Gates, Jr.,
quotes a figure of nearly 300,000. A version of Gates's lecture appears
as "Whose Canon Is It, Anyway?" in the *New York Times Book Review*
(February 26, 1989): 1, 44–45. In addition to Gates, the 1989 lecture

Introduction

series featured versions of the essays in this volume by Hazel Carby, Rachel DuPlessis, Robert Hemenway, and Nellie McKay, and a lecture/reading by the novelist Gloria Naylor, "Zora Neale Hurston and My Search for a Sense of Place." I want to take this occasion to thank the participants; the King/Chavez/Parks Visiting Minority Professor Program, the Rackham School of Graduate Studies, and the College of Literature, Science, and the Arts, whose monetary contributions made the lecture series possible; those members of the University of Michigan community whose assistance was especially important: Carol Barash, Don Belton, Gerri Brewer, June Howard, Lemuel Johnson, Richard Meisler, Gloria Parsons, Martha Vicinus, Bob Weisbuch, and Sue Williams; and the intelligent, enthusiastic graduate students enrolled in my Winter Term 1989 course on Afro-American women novelists. Also, I wish to thank Katie O'Connell for her assistance with the preparation of this volume.

8. Quoted in Alice Walker, "Looking for Zora," *In Search of Our Mothers' Gardens* (San Diego: Harcourt Brace Jovanovich, 1983), p. 106.
9. See Robert Hemenway, *Zora Neale Hurston: A Literary Biography* (Urbana: University of Illinois Press, 1977); Houston A. Baker, Jr., *Blues, Ideology, and Afro-American Literature* (Chicago: University of Chicago Press, 1984), pp. 57–60; Callahan, "'Mah Tongue Is in Mah Friend's Mouf': The Rhetoric of Intimacy and Immensity in *Their Eyes Were Watching God*," *In the African American Grain*, pp. 115–49; and Gates, *The Signifying Monkey*, pp. 170–216.
10. See Marjorie Pryse, "Zora Neale Hurston, Alice Walker, and the 'Ancient Power' of Black Women," in *Conjuring: Black Women, Fiction, and Literary Tradition*, ed. Marjorie Pryse and Hortense J. Spillers (Bloomington: Indiana University Press, 1985), pp. 1–24; Elizabeth Meese, "Orality and Textuality in *Their Eyes Were Watching God*," *Crossing the Double-Cross: The Practice of Feminist Criticism* (Chapel Hill: University of North Carolina Press, 1986), pp. 39–54; and Susan Willis, "Wandering: Zora Neale Hurston's Search for Self and Method," *Specifying: Black Women Writing the American Experience* (Madison: University of Wisconsin Press, 1987), pp. 26–52.
11. See, for example, Emory Elliott, gen. ed., *Columbia Literary History of the United States*, (New York: Columbia University Press, 1988); Harold Bloom, ed., *Modern Critical Interpretations: "Their Eyes Were Watching God"* (New York: Chelsea House Publishers, 1987); Bloom, ed., *Modern Critical Views: Zora Neale Hurston* (New York: Chelsea House Publishers, 1986); and Bloom, ed., *American Fiction 1914 to 1945* (New York: Chelsea House Publishers, 1986), which contains (as

23

do the Hurston volumes) Barbara Johnson's "Metaphor, Metonymy, and Voice in *Their Eyes Were Watching God,*" pp. 361–74. Bloom's introduction to the Hurston volumes suggests that he is not thoroughly persuaded by the feminist and Afrocentric essays on *Their Eyes Were Watching God* which he includes. He says in his introduction: "Hurston herself was refreshingly free of all the ideologies that currently obscure the reception of her best book" (4). The implications of Bloom's figuring of an ideology-less Hurston have been discussed in Michele Wallace, "Who Dat Say Who Dat When I Say Who Dat?: Zora Neale Hurston Then and Now," *The Village Voice Literary Supplement* (April 1988): 18–19, and Michael Awkward, "Race, Gender, and the Politics of Reading," *Black American Literature Forum* 22 (1988): 13–15.

12. Barbara Christian, "Trajectories of Self-Definition: Placing Contemporary Afro-American Women's Fiction," in *Conjuring,* p. 137. See also Christian, *Black Women Novelists* (Westport, CT: Greenwood Press, 1980); Barbara Smith, "Toward a Black Feminist Criticism" in *The New Feminist Criticism,* ed. Elaine Showalter (New York: Pantheon, 1985), pp. 168–85; and Mary Helen Washington, *Invented Lives: Narratives of Black Women 1860–1960* (Garden City, NJ: Doubleday, 1987).

13. Henry Louis Gates, Jr., "A Negro Way of Saying," *New York Times Book Review* (April 21, 1985): 43.

14. Alice Walker, *Mothers' Gardens,* p. 86. Essays in this volume in which Walker comments on Hurston include "Saving the Life That Is Your Own: The Importance of Models in the Artist's Life," pp. 3–14; "Zora Neale Hurston: A Cautionary Tale and a Partisan View," pp. 83–92; "Looking for Zora," pp. 93–116; "In Search of Our Mothers' Gardens," pp. 231–43; and "If the Present Looks Like the Past, What Does the Future Look Like?" pp. 290–312. These essays provide one of the most fascinating accounts in American literary history of a writer's engagement in the works of an artistic forebear. Critical texts that explore intertextual relationships between the two most acclaimed novels of these writers, Walker's *The Color Purple* and Hurston's *Their Eyes Were Watching God,* include Deborah McDowell, "'The Changing Same': Generational Connections and Black Women Novelists," *New Literary History* 18 (1986): 281–302; Michael Awkward, "*The Color Purple* and the Achievement of (Comm)unity," *Inspiriting Influences,* pp. 135–64; Marjorie Pryse, "Zora Neale Hurston, Alice Walker," *Conjuring,* pp. 1–24; Diane F. Sadoff, "Black Matrilineage: The Case of Alice Walker and Zora Neale Hurston," *Signs* 11 (1985): 4–26; and Henry Louis Gates, Jr., "Color Me Zora: Alice

Walker's (Re)Writing of the Speakerly Text," *The Signifying Monkey,* pp. 239–58.

15. Sherley Anne Williams, "Foreword," *Their Eyes Were Watching God,* pp. v–xv; Toni Cade Bambara, "Some Forward Remarks," Hurston, *The Sanctified Church* (Berkeley: Turtle Island Foundation, 1983), pp. 7–11; Gloria Naylor, "Zora Neale Hurston," and Terry McMillan, *Disappearing Acts* (New York: Viking, 1989). *Their Eyes Were Watching God* is the favorite novel of McMillan's female protagonist, whose name, Zora Banks, is a conflation of Hurston's first name and the surname of a female character of Hurston's short story, "The Gilded Six-Bits."

16. George Stevens, "Negroes by Themselves," *Saturday Review of Literature* (September 18, 1937): 3; Herschel Brickell, review of *Their Eyes Were Watching God,* the *New York Post* (September 14, 1937), discussed in Hemenway, *Zora Neale Hurston,* p. 241.

17. Hemenway, *Zora Neale Hurston,* p. 4.

18. Ibid., p. 6.

19. Robert Bone, *The Negro Novel in America* (New Haven: Yale University Press, 1965), p. 128.

20. Julius Lester, *Black Folktales* (New York: Grove Press, 1969); June Jordan, "On Richard Wright and Zora Neale Hurston: Notes Toward a Balancing of Love and Hatred," *Black World* (August 1974): 6; Larry Neal, "Eatonville's Zora Neale Hurston: A Profile," *Visions of a Liberated Future: Black Arts Movement Writings* (New York: Thunder's Mouth Press, 1989), p. 88; Roger Whitlow, *Black American Literature: A Critical History* (1974. Totowa, NJ: Rowman and Allanheld, 1984), p. 106; and Addison Gayle, *The Way of the New World: The Black Novel in America* (Garden City, NY: Anchor Press, 1975), p. 178.

21. Gates, *The Signifying Monkey,* p. 180.

22. Barbara Herrnstein Smith, *Contingencies of Value: Alternative Perspectives for Critical Theory* (Cambridge, MA: Harvard University Press, 1988), p. 30.

23. John Raeburn, "Skirting the Hemingway Legend," *American Literary History* 1 (1989): 208.

24. Smith, *Contingencies of Value,* p. 49.

25. Langston Hughes, "The Negro Artist and the Racial Mountain," *Five Black Writers,* ed. Donald Gibson (New York: New York University Press, 1970), p. 225.

26. Wright, "Between Laughter and Tears," pp. 22, 25, my emphasis.

27. I am intentionally employing Wright's image in *Native Son* of blindness, of an inability to see beyond surface appearances and biased

preconceptions, and turning the charge against Wright for his response to Hurston. See Wright, *Native Son* (New York: Harper and Row, 1940).

28. Carl Milton Hughes, *The Negro Novelist* (New York: Citadel Press, 1953), p. 172.

29. Barbara Johnson used this phrase to describe Richard Wright's androcentricism in "Metaphor, Metonymy, and Voice in *Their Eyes Were Watching God*," *A World of Difference* (Baltimore: Johns Hopkins University Press, 1987), p. 167. Johnson observes that Wright's interpretative blindness resulted from a general human difficulty to see beyond differences: "[T]he full range of questions and experiences of Janie's life are as invisible to a mind steeped in maleness as Ellison's *Invisible Man* is to minds steeped in whiteness" (167). As we have seen, those characteristics that Johnson identifies as sources of interpretative blindness – race and gender – serve in varying degrees to delimit the nature and, to some extent, the quality of early responses to Hurston.

30. Langston Hughes, "The Negro Artist," p. 226. For discussions of the Hurston–Hughes fallout over "Mule Bone," see Hughes, *The Big Sea* (New York: Hill and Wang, 1940), pp. 320, 331–4; Hemenway, *Zora Neale Hurston*, pp. 136–58; David Levering Lewis, *When Harlem Was in Vogue* (New York: Vintage, 1981), pp. 257, 260–1; and Arnold Rampersad, *The Life of Langston Hughes, Vol. I: 1902–1941* (New York: Oxford University Press, 1986), pp. 182–200. Although varying in some degree about the amount of malicious intent that characterized the act – Hemenway's account is the most sympathetic to Hurston – all of these commentators agree that Hurston was at fault for trying to pass off this cowritten play as solely her own composition. Curiously, but perhaps not surprisingly, Hurston does not mention this affair in her autobiography, *Dust Tracks on a Road*, and she virtually ignores Langston Hughes and the Harlem Renaissance altogether.

31. Langston Hughes, *The Big Sea*, pp. 238–9.

32. See Wallace Thurman, *Infants of the Spring* (New York: Macaulay, 1932); Nathan Huggins, *Harlem Renaissance* (New York: Oxford University Press, 1971), pp. 130–3; and Darwin Turner, "Zora Neale Hurston: The Wandering Minstrel," *In a Minor Chord* (Carbondale: Southern Illinois University Press, 1971), pp. 89–120.

33. Jordan, "Between Laughter and Tears," pp. 4, 5.

34. Walker, "Zora Neale Hurston," p. 86.

35. Lloyd W. Brown, "Zora Neale Hurston and the Nature of Female Perception," *Obsidian* 4 (1978): 39.

Introduction

36. Robert Hemenway, *Zora Neale Hurston*, p. 232.
37. Robert Stepto, *From Behind the Veil* (Urbana: University of Illinois Press, 1979), p. 166.
38. See Bernard Bell, *The Afro-American Novel and Its Tradition* (Amherst: University of Massachusetts Press, 1987), pp. 121–7; Lillie Howard, "Nanny and Janie: Will the Twain Ever Meet?" *Journal of Black Studies* 12 (1982): 403–14. Bell, for example, who argues that one of the novel's major problems is its "awkward handling of point of view," insists that the protagonist's failure to assume control over the story-telling by providing her first person narration "diminishes the reader's emotional involvement with and moral sympathy for Janie" (p. 123).
39. Callahan, "Mah Tongue Is in Mah Friend's Mouf," pp. 117–18.
40. See Hazel Carby, *Reconstructing Womanhood: The Emergence of the Afro-American Woman Novelist* (New York: Oxford University Press, 1987); Rachel Blau DuPlessis, *Writing beyond the Ending: Narrative Strategies of Twentieth-Century Women Writers* (Bloomington: Indiana University Press, 1985), pp. 156–8; Robert Hemenway, *Zora Neale Hurston;* and Nellie McKay, "Race, Gender, and Cultural Context in Zora Neale Hurston's *Dust Tracks on a Road*," in *Life/Lines: Theorizing Women's Autobiography*, ed. Bella Brodzki and Celeste Schenck (Ithaca: Cornell University Press, 1988), pp. 175–88.
41. Nathan Huggins, *Harlem Renaissance*, p. 74.
42. Alain Locke, "Jingo, Counter-Jingo and Us," p. 10.

2

The Personal Dimension in
Their Eyes Were Watching God

ROBERT HEMENWAY

1

I APPROACH the task of discussing Zora Neale Hurston here with considerable humility. Since *Zora Neale Hurston: A Literary Biography* was published, I have been five years a department head, three years a dean, and am now a chancellor. There are many days when my contribution to the March of Knowledge comes not from scholarship, but from an ingenious scheme for financing the asbestos abatement.

The distinguished company here is intimidating, because it is fair to say that all other writers in this volume are younger than I am, and all have been trained as critical theorists in a way that my generation of scholars was not.

I came to professional literary consciousness in the last wave – really the last gasp – of New Criticism. The Olympian canon was an object of worship, and African-American texts were, by definition, considered inferior objects of study, a category of primitive artifact, exotically interesting, but of a different order from the sacred canon of the high church of American literature.

The training of that particular generation – my generation – has now been superseded, left behind in the dust after the explosion of theory that has reinvigorated our profession. It has been a very liberating experience for me and for the texts I interpret, like *Their Eyes Were Watching God*. I no longer have to bite my tongue when a colleague states, as one of my colleagues said to me only five years ago, "Well, the Hurston book was interesting, and so is *Their Eyes*, but I hope you'll take on a *major figure* next time."

When I first began studying Zora Neale Hurston, I found that, like my mugwumpish colleague who advised working with a major figure, no one wanted to grant much importance to a text like *Their Eyes Were Watching God*. Lately, I have noticed a tendency to let *Their Eyes Were Watching God*, and Hurston, into the canon, but only on very special terms.

Canon formation in the dying days of professional modernism has assumed the shape of the academic rank system, a status–value system that assumes the work of full professors to be, by definition, of greater value than that of assistant professors. Thus, scholars have suggested an equal-opportunity canon where all are included, but some authors are more important than others. All "qualified" applicants, regardless of race, are eligible to enter the canon, but most minorities (and women) cluster at the lowest (read "assistant professor") levels, whereas the upper ranks, (read "full professors") remain predominantly white, male, and relatively free of the coming and going of literary reputations. The lower ranks, meanwhile, being more inclusive, tend to see a lot of substitution (a situation presumably analogous to the coming and going of assistant professors in the search for tenure).

Under this EEO merit-system canon, Melville's place is secure, a full professor surely. Hemingway is good, but not of the first rank (an associate professor, who seems to repeat himself). Zora Neale Hurston has a precarious hold at the untenured assistant professor level – the jury being still out on the nature of her achievement – and is subject to replacement by Jamaica Kincaid or some other promising newcomer.

I am being personal here because I have learned from the theory revolution the importance of situating oneself as a critic, of becoming *self-conscious* about the intellectual assumptions brought to the act of interpretation. Cary Nelson's fine collection, *Theory in the Classroom*, a set of essays that demonstrates critical theory's relationship to the act of professing literature, has made me particularly aware of this self-consciousness. As he puts it in his introduction: "In these essays there is *a recurrent will to self-reflection*" (my italics).[1]

In Nelson's own essay in the collection, he lists 79 interrogatives, all of which emphasize the acute self-consciousness that a modern interpreter brings to the text. He asks questions such as:

1. Do interpreters seek power over the objects they interpret? Over other interpreters?
2. Does an individual's subjectivity determine how, or what, he or she interprets? In what way? To what degree? Does the act of interpretation itself determine subjectivity?
3. How is difference (sexual, racial, class, national identity) inscribed in interpretation?
4. To what degree do interpretative communities control the nature of interpretation?[2]

All of these questions reflect Nelson's "recurrent will to self-reflection." You cannot ask yourself such questions without becoming self-conscious. Do I seek power over others? No teacher, writer, dean, or chancellor can be at ease with the question.

What I wish to do is read *Their Eyes* through an analogous prism of self-consciousness – my light source, however feeble it may be, emanating first from Hurston's personal and literary history, and second from *Their Eyes* as a self-conscious text. I will try to focus on Hurston's self-consciousness in presenting folklore as the sign of cultural difference in the novel.

I want to suggest, first, that my generation of literary scholars has distorted both Hurston's life and art, and has especially distorted the way we contextualize *Their Eyes* within literary history. Second, I want to suggest that my generation of interpreters, in confronting literary theory and being made self-conscious about the act of interpretation, has experienced something like what Zora Neale Hurston went through in her struggle to dramatize folklore as a sign of cultural difference, a boundary demarcating race.

2

The Harlem Renaissance constitutes a perfect unit of literary history. It is the answer to an anthologist's dreams.[3] As a label it has instant product identification; it implies ethnic movement and lit-

31

erary rebirth. Out of the chaos of the Roaring Twenties and the "jazz age," the "Harlem Renaissance" suggests order and common purpose.

Scholars have jumped at the chance to classify African-American writers within a limited historical period (usually 1919–29) rooted in a particular geographical space (Harlem) and committed to a presumed common goal ("New Negroism"). More analysis of the Harlem Renaissance has been published than for any other period in African-American literary history. More may have been written about the Harlem Renaissance than about the rest of African-American literature combined.

For individual writers this emphasis on the Harlem Renaissance results in an overemphasis on that part of the author's career that falls within the period boundaries. Thus, Arna Bontemps is often discussed as a Harlem Renaissance poet, although his ideas and methods were largely shaped during the 1930s and 1940s in his major work – almost all of it in prose. (When I first met Arna in the early 1970s, he sometimes complained about the fact that his identification with the Harlem Renaissance, fifty years earlier, caused everyone now to presume that he was dead.)

Zora Neale Hurston's career has also been distorted because of her classification as a "Renaissance" author. Hurston failed to achieve artistic success until relatively late in life, during the Great Depression, with *Their Eyes*. Even to label Hurston a Harlem Renaissance artist places considerable burden on her meager writing during the period. Her major achievements, *Mules and Men* (1935) and *Their Eyes Were Watching God* (1937), the two works that confirm her reputation as an important American writer, could almost certainly *not* have been written during the 1920s. Although the flamboyant Zora maintained a vivid presence during the Harlem Renaissance, and was remembered by all, her work did not reach maturity until she freed herself from the anxieties of literary patronage. During the Harlem Renaissance, Hurston suffered, sometimes because of her own actions, from the peculiar burdens white wealth bestows upon black artists.

What Hurston possessed during the Renaissance decade was a career in patronage. Studies of the period have filled the void left by her lack of writing with accounts of that patronage, with the result that her success in securing support has received close scrutiny and considerable criticism. Nathan Huggins, Darwin Turner, and David Levering Lewis have all questioned the role Hurston assumed with her patrons.[4] Yet it is worth remembering that Hurston was only one among many young black artists who found a patron. What was different about her was the lack of a body of work to deflect attention away from the money.

In the scholar's periodic march through African-American literary history from the Harlem Renaissance to the Black Arts Movement, Hurston's achievement becomes paradoxical. Critics acknowledge the achievement of *Their Eyes Were Watching God*, finding it a magnificent affirmation of her ability, yet consider the success surprising, given her relationships with white patrons during the spotlighted years of the Renaissance. The patronage arrangements of the 1920s inevitably affect the view of Hurston's total career, and the approach to *Their Eyes*.

Those patronage arrangements during the Harlem Renaissance should be placed in the perspective of her later success. Hurston received major financial support for seven years, beginning in 1925, from three rich and powerful white women. It was the only time in her life she systematically received private patronage. It also proved to her, I think, that such patronage could not contribute to the peace of mind, nor generate the creative energy, nor create the sense of audience she needed to become a successful writer.

Some have argued that Hurston's early career as a protégée of whites tarnished her image and cheapened her talent, casting a shadow over later achievement. All of Hurston's major work was published *after* the patronage period, a fact provoking the following question: Did the influence of white patronage persist once the money stopped? Is *Their Eyes Were Watching God*, for example, tainted or compromised by the patronage that ended five years prior to its publication?

Between 1925 and 1932, Zora Neale Hurston had three patrons: Annie Nathan Meyer, daughter of one of the oldest Jewish families in New York City, and a founder of Barnard College; Fannie Hurst, the best selling novelist of the 1920s and 1930s, known for her novel of passing, *Imitation of Life*; and the mysterious, powerful,

Mrs. R. Osgood Mason, patron to such other Harlem Renaissance artists as Langston Hughes, Alain Locke, Richmond Barthe, Aaron Douglass, and Claude McKay.

Hurston's correspondence with these patrons – largely unknown previously and now available at the University of Texas, Howard University, and Cincinnati's Hebrew Union Archive – reveals that the Meyer and Hurst patronages have been misunderstood, and that the Mason patronage created much more anxiety than previously reported. Zora's three patrons of 1925–32 were wealthy New Yorkers, active in the arts, who were part of the philanthropic pipeline that led to the NAACP. While being supported by one or the other for almost a decade, Hurston managed to graduate from Barnard and conduct the fieldwork in African-American folk culture which became the basis for much of her career.

Hurston's support during her early years in New York from 1925 to 1927 is easily sketched. Annie Nathan Meyer, Barnard trustee, arranged for her admission, and provided sums for living expenses, never entirely paying for room, board, or tuition. Fannie Hurst employed her for a short time as a secretary (less than two months), occasionally thereafter as a driver and companion. Impressed with her grades but put off by her volatile personality, Barnard College reluctantly granted her a scholarship for two of her three semesters. Zora partially supported herself by freelance writing, part-time anthropology jobs, loans from other benefactors (both black and white), and day work for families whom Mrs. Meyer contacted on her behalf. In other words, *Hurston received less support during her Barnard years than most college athletes.* To think of Mrs. Meyer or Fannie Hurst as "patrons" in the classic sense distorts their friendship with Hurston.

The relationship with Mrs. Mason is more complicated. I have written elsewhere of this arrangement, but the outlines are clear.[5] Hurston met Mrs. Mason in September 1927, after her return to New York following completion of a fellowship from the Association for the Study of Negro Life and History. In December 1927, she signed a contract of employment with Mrs. Mason which provided for $200 per month, a motion picture camera, and an automobile, so that Hurston could collect folklore in the South for the next two years. The folklore collected was to be considered Mrs. Mason's property. Eventually, Mason supported Hurston until September of 1932, cutting off funds after Zora failed to complete a publishable draft of *Mules and Men*.

I am not going to detail the subtleties of the Mason–Hurston relations, but Mrs. Mason's effect on Hurston is easily documented from the correspondence between them available at the Moorland–Spingarn collection at Howard University. In the two years of extant correspondence with her patron, Zora complained of tonsillitis, depression, "dust in the head," flu, a "sick soul," disorganization, "no lamp within," disillusionment, colon trouble, intestinal ailments, burnt-out nerves, and "befogged vision." She felt the pressure day after day, and it destroyed her work. Between 1927 and 1932, the years of the Mason patronage, Hurston wrote no fiction, first because she was collecting, later because she was struggling with *Mules and Men* under the Mason eye. After she returned from the South in 1929, and began to live within easy reach of Mrs. Mason's call, her depression was considerable. The reduction in the Mason stipend from $200 per month to half that amount in 1931 exemplifies the pressure she worked under.

All of this Harlem Renaissance patronage occurred prior to Hurston's successful writing career. Between November 1926 and August 1933 – seven years coinciding almost exactly to the patronage period – Hurston published no fiction. Her only significant publication during this period, "Hoodoo in America," published by the *Journal of American Folklore* in December 1931, was more a compilation of folklore fieldwork than creative achievement.

This evidence suggests that Zora Neale Hurston could not write creatively while under the influence of personal patronage. Once freed of the anxieties that seem to accompany such gifts, Hurston's greatest work began. In the decade following the final break with Mrs. Mason, Hurston published six of her seven books, a long series of essays in Nancy Cunard's *Negro,* and a large number of reviews, short stories, and essays. Something about being on her own, even if it meant scrambling for every hard-earned dollar, liberated Hurston's imagination. She never went back to a personal patronage relationship, and her career was never again mortgaged on the promise of her talent.

I believe that Hurston sensed, later in the patronage period, that something about the gift giving had inhibited her talent. My primary evidence is that only in the release that came with the creation of *Jonah's Gourd Vine* – a novel which she proudly explained was written under the direst poverty in 1933[6] – did she enter into the mature achievement leading to *Their Eyes Were Watching God.* Does this mean that *Their Eyes* is free of the patronage influence? In one sense, yes; in another, no.

It has always been assumed that white patronage has a negative effect on black writers.[7] This was certainly Langston Hughes's position, and there is considerable evidence to suggest that he was right. But patronage can also give a writer a counterforce, a foil that forces the writer into articulating the *difference* between his or her environment and that of the patron. Thus, Hughes's anticapitalist poems forced the break with Mrs. Mason.[8]

What patronage did for Zora Neale Hurston was to force her to define the role of black folklore, in her life and in her fiction, much more clearly than she had ever done before. Patronage made Hurston *self-conscious* about her role as the dramatist for something unique about black American experience – the rich folklore of rural black Southerners.

Hurston's relations with her patrons – especially with Mrs. Mason, where her knowledge of folklore led her to a situation where she was always expected to *be black culture,* to represent the difference that was blackness – prefigure some of her major concerns in *Their Eyes Were Watching God.*

White Americans have expected African-American artists from Phillis Wheatley to James Baldwin to Toni Morrison to Alice Walker to explain, as Zora once put it, "How It Feels To Be Colored Me." This is the cultural equivalent to the tiresome political question asked of black leaders in the 1940s, "What does the Negro want?"

This kind of interlocutionary discourse is often explicitly or implicitly present in black writing. *Their Eyes Were Watching God* generally uses folkloric discourse to answer such questions. Indeed, one way to view this text is as Hurston's answer to the question, How does it feel to be a black woman? As a result, one way to approach the novel is through Hurston's 1929 essay, "How It Feels

To Be Colored Me," an essay written in the midst of the patronage period and published in *The World Tomorrow* in May of 1928.[9]

Barbara Johnson, in an acute analysis of this essay, points out that Hurston could often proclaim "I am this" in answer to "how it feels to be colored me," but when the image is repeated as "You are that," the interlocutionary moment changes completely. Johnson generalizes that "[t]he study of Afro-American literature as a whole poses a similar problem of address: any attempt to lift out of a text an image or essence of blackness is bound to violate the interlocutionary strategy of its foundation." Johnson goes on to explain that "[f]ar from answering how it feels to be colored me, Hurston deconstructs the very grounds of an answer, replying 'Compared to what? As of when? Who is asking? In what context? For what purpose?'"[10]

Johnson's set of interrogatives are similar to Cary Nelson's. They suggest that Hurston brought to such questions a certain level of self-consciousness. Hurston's self-consciousness demonstrates the wisdom of Henry Louis Gates's understanding of black use of the figurative:

> Black people have always been masters of the figurative: saying one thing to mean something quite other has been basic to black survival in oppressive Western cultures. Misreading signs could be, and indeed often was, fatal. "Reading," in this sense, was not play; it was an essential aspect of "literacy" training of a child. This sort of metaphysical literacy, the learning to decipher complex codes [I would add the ability to deconstruct such questions as "How Does It Feel To Be Colored You?"] is just about the blackest aspect of the black tradition.[11]

I provide this background as an introduction to the reader's opportunity to hear Zora Neale Hurston speak about these kinds of topics.

In the summer of 1935, Zora Neale Hurston traveled across the South on a folklore-collecting trip with Alan Lomax and a college professor named Mary Elizabeth Barnicle. They were all working for the Library of Congress. Lomax recorded Hurston singing folksongs, and the tape of that recording now resides in the folklore archive of the Library of Congress. It is revealing for two important reasons: First, as far as I know, it is the only surviving recording of Zora Neale Hurston talking; and second, recorded only two years before *Their Eyes Were Watching God* was written, the tape illustrates the role Hurston played, as a folklore collector and artist, in the interlocutionary discourse about race which arises when black folklore becomes the object of interpretation, or when it is dramatized for a general audience.

The transcription of a short selection from this tape provides a context for my brief reading of a specific folkloric scene in *Their Eyes Were Watching God*. The questions here are being asked by Alan Lomax, who becomes a kind of interlocutor. Lomax and Hurston were good friends, but his questions still have the effect of making her self-conscious. She is in the process of defining difference, and Lomax wants to know her credentials. How does she know these songs? How does she learn them? Implicitly, what do you know that white folks do not? Implicitly, what is special or unique about African-American culture?[12]

Hurston: "Oh the Buford Boat done come" is a song from the Geechee country in South Carolina but I heard it done in Florida from a Geechee that had moved down in Florida. I forget her name right now.

Lomax: What kind of song is it?

Hurston: It is a little dance song and it has that Charleston rhythm . . .

Lomax: How is it played? Could you tell me very quickly?

Hurston: It's just a dance song, and then they dance a Charleston rhythm on it.

Lomax: Is it solo dancing?

Hurston: No, it's group dancing.

Lomax: Well what kind of group?

Hurston: Oh, just any working group and they'll clap their hands on it and sing . . .

Hurston: I'm going to sing a blues called "Ever Been Down" and I got it at Palm Beach from a fellow named Johnny Darden.

Lomax: When did you get it?

Hurston: I got it in 1933.

Lomax: Do you know how old of blues it is? Or where he happened to learn it?

Hurston: Well it's just one of those things that just go around all of the jooks and what not like that and grows by incremental repetition. I don't suppose anybody knows just how old it is and when it started . . .

Hurston: I heard "Halimuhfack" down on the East Coast.
Lomax: Who did you here it from and when?
Hurston: I don't remember. I was in a big crowd and I learned it in the
evening during the crowd and just can't remember who did
teach it to me. I learned it from the crowd . . .
Lomax: You said you learned it in a crowd. Where do you learn most of
your songs?
Hurston: I just get in the crowd with the people when they sing it, I listen
as best I can, then I start to join in with a phrase or two and then
finally I get so that I can sing a verse. Then I keep on till I learn
all of the songs with verses then I sing 'em back to the people till
they tell me that I can sing them just like them and then I take
part and try it out on different people who already know the
song until they are quite satisfied that I know it, and then I carry
it in my memory.
Lomax: How about those that are in your books and are published in
your journals?
Hurston: Well, that's the same way I got them. I learned the song myself,
and then I can take it with me wherever I go . . .
Hurston: This is a song called "Tampa." I've known it ever since I could
remember so I don't know who taught it to me but I heard it
sung in my native village when I was a child, not in front of the
old folks, of course.
Lomax: When was that sung?
Hurston: I've known it all my life, so it was not confined to children.
Everybody sung and danced on it and you hear Negro orchestras or local orchestras often play it now. Play the tune, they
don't sing the words, but the tune is one of the very favorite
dance tunes . . .[13]

With this dialogue in mind, I want to finish by focusing on one
particular scene in *Their Eyes Were Watching God*, which in some
ways assumes an interlocutory situation not all that different from
the tape. What the scene shows, I think, is what Barbara Johnson
concluded from her analysis of "How It Feels To Be Colored Me":
"[Q]uestions of difference and identity are always a function of a
specific interlocutionary situation – and the answers, matters of
strategy rather than truth."[14]

3

I want to concentrate on the rather bizarre episode of Matt Bonner's Yellow Mule, which is not even central to the narrative, but

New Essays on Their Eyes Were Watching God

which provides a window for viewing the entire novel – especially the way in which folklore becomes the line of demarcation between self and other, between black and white, between women and men, between participant culture-making and observed culture.

The cantankerous yellow mule of *Their Eyes Were Watching God* serves as a constant source of inspiration for the group of storytellers who inhabit the front porch of Eatonville's general store. This store porch and its storytellers are absolutely central to Hurston's creative imagination. They are the "big picture talkers" who use the "side of the world for a canvas" (85), creating "crayon enlargements of life." They function as a kind of chorus in *Their Eyes Were Watching God*, and also appear in *Jonah's Gourd Vine*, *Mules and Men* and *Dust Tracks on a Road*.

This yellow mule in *Their Eyes Were Watching God* is a profound conversational presence to Eatonville's verbal artists, Sam, Lige, and Walter, who are the "ring leaders of the mule talkers," and who "had him up for conversation every day the Lord sent" (48). He is a mule so skinny that the women "is usin' his rib bones fuh uh rub-board and hangin' things out on his hock-bones to dry." He's so mean he refuses to get fat, staying "poor and rawbony jus' fuh spite" (49). He is the kind of mule who stuck his head in the Pearsons' window while the family was at the dinner table, and whom Mrs. Pearson mistook for the Reverend and handed a plate. He is the kind of mule who slept in the Lindsays' kitchen one night and the next morning "fought until they made coffee for his breakfast" (55). All in all, fourteen pages of *Their Eyes Were Watching God* are taken up with the yellow mule.

When the yellow mule dies in *Their Eyes Were Watching God*, the town buries him in an elaborate ceremony which, Hurston tells us, "mocked everything human in death." At the funeral, they speak of "the joys of mule heaven to which the dear brother had departed this valley of sorrow." They speak of mule angels flying around in miles of green corn and drinking in cool water, and report that in Mule Heaven, mule angels will have "people to ride on" (57).

Finally, after much ceremony, the town leaves the mule to the buzzards, who have been sitting in nearby trees, waiting:

Everybody enjoyed themselves to the highest and then finally the mule was left to the already impatient buzzards. They were holding great flying-meet way up over the heads of the mourners and some of the nearby trees were already peopled with the stoop-shouldered forms.

As soon as the crowd was out of sight they closed in in circles. The near ones got nearer and the far ones got near. A circle, a swoop and a hop with spread-out wings. Close in, close in till some of the more hungry or daring perched on the carcass. They wanted to begin, but the Parson wasn't there, so a messenger was sent to the ruler in a tree where he sat.

The flock had to wait the white-headed leader, but it was hard. They jostled each other and pecked at heads in hungry irritation. Some walked up and down the beast from head to tail, tail to head. The Parson sat motionless in a dead pine tree about two miles off. He had scented the matter as quickly as any of the rest, but decorum demanded that he sit oblivious until he was notified. Then he took off with ponderous flight and circled and lowered, circled and lowered until the others danced in joy and hunger at his approach.

He finally lit on the ground and walked around the body to see if it were really dead. Peered into its nose and mouth. Examined it well from end to end and leaped upon it and bowed, and the others *danced* a response. That being over, he balanced and asked:

> "What killed this man?"
> The chorus answered, "Bare, bare fat."
> "What killed this man?"
> "Bare, bare fat."
> "Who'll stand his funeral?"
> "We!!!!!"
> "Well, all right now."

So he picked out the eyes in the ceremonial way and the feast went on. The yaller mule was gone from the town except for the porch talk, and for the children visiting his bleaching bones now and then in the spirit of adventure. (57–8)

This is a very strange scene, one that Henry Louis Gates calls "The Allegory of the Buzzards," an allegory that he says "shatters completely any illusion the reader might have had that this was meant to be realistic fiction."[15] It has often been cited as a good example of the way that Hurston permits her sense of folklore to impose itself on her fiction. There are no other talking animals anywhere in the novel, and *Their Eyes Were Watching God* is definitely not a phantasmagoric text, such as *One Hundred Years of Solitude,* where flower petals fall from the sky with about as much warning as these buzzards begin to talk. The scene is obviously an allegory of the mock burial that precedes it, complete with a Parson presiding at the center of the ceremony.

Another section of the Lomax–Hurston tape provides a provocative means of thinking about the speaking buzzards in *Their Eyes Were Watching God:*

Hurston: [This is a] game that evidently has come from Africa. Dr. Herskovits says that he saw the background of it in West Africa, of the crow. The crow in some way seems to be sacred in Africa. But what they are talking about [is] what we know in the United States as the buzzard and the buzzard comes to get something to eat and they are talking about [it] and they dance it. And one person gets in the center and imitates the buzzard and the rest of them form the background.

Song

Oh, my Mama come see that crow
See how she flies
Oh, Mama come see that crow
See how she flies

This crow, this crow goin' fly tonight,
See how he flies
This crow, this crow goin' fly tonight,
See how he flies

Oh, my Mama come see that crow
See how he flies
Oh, Mama come see that crow
See how he flies

This crow, this crow goin' fly tonight
See how he flies
This crow, this crow goin' fly tonight
See how he flies

Oh, Mama come see that crow
Caaaa
Oh, Mama come see that crow
Caaaa

The Personal Dimension

Oh, my Mama come see that crow
See how he flies

This Archive of Folksong recording gives us another perspective on the buzzard scene in *Their Eyes Were Watching God*. Hurston had knowledge of a Crow Dance, the image and words of which she carried with her wherever she went, and she identified West Indian or African crows as buzzards in the United States. Understood in this context, the buzzards became representative folk figures, symbols of communal cohesion, an example of the sense of narrative that makes Eatonville different.

Matt Bonner's mule and the burial ceremony document a creative culture which Janie Starks is a part of, but in which she has been denied the rights of expression by her husband, the mayor. Even buzzards have a role in the rhythm of nature honored in Eatonville, but Janie does not. Hurston tells us, "Janie loved the conversation and sometimes she thought up good stories on the mule, but Joe had forbidden her to indulge. He didn't want her talking after such trashy people" (50).

Janie is also not allowed to attend the mule's funeral, since the mayor's wife is "someone who shouldn't be seen at uh dragging out . . . wid any and everybody in uh passle pushin' and shovin' wid they no manners selves" (56). As the mule is dragged away, Hurston reports: "the town escorted the carcass off. No, the carcass moved off with the town, and left Janie standing in the doorway" (57). The rest of the novel documents Janie's search to liberate herself from a world that imposes artificial distinctions of class, a world that imposes male fantasies of socialization that deny women the right to autonomous decisions. It also shows Janie seeking her place – and her voice – in the African-American community as an individual woman, a task that becomes a struggle to live as something other than "de mule uh de world" (14), which her grandmother claims is the lot of the black woman.

Both the yellow mule and the buzzards convey a sense of imaginative freedom. A community that confers humanity on an ugly yellow mule and a novelist who lets some local buzzards talk their talk reveal a special kind of capacity for narrative improvisation. Janie Starks, the narrator of the novel, is eventually able to tell her story because she reclaims her communal narrative endowment,

43

an oral tradition that ignores the representational boundaries of fact and fiction, and documents a complex system of cultural communication that we label black folklore. In short, Janie reclaims the ability to deconstruct the question, "How Does It Feel To Be Colored You," through the medium of black folklore.

What has never been adequately studied in either *Their Eyes Were Watching God*, or in African-American fiction generally, is the way that folklore empowers one to deconstruct that interlocutionary moment. Oral tradition crosses over into written expression, carrying with it the complex meanings and special cultural functions that make African-American narrative such a triumph of the human imagination. During slavery and Reconstruction, black people created a special narrative tradition that provided unique forms and unique subjects for the act and art of storytelling, and the act and art of establishing personal and group identity. Embodied in spirituals, heroic legends, proverbs, and traditional jokes, but especially in folktales, the tradition became a reservoir of figurative language that helped black people survive and affirm themselves as culturally unique.

Time after time in *Their Eyes Were Watching God*, Hurston tries to represent the "difference" of blackness through a representation of the folk process. That is why talking buzzards, a ceremonial yellow mule, big picture talkers on Joe Clarke's Store porch, Bahamian Fire Dancers, and lying sessions in the Muck appear so frequently. It is why there is such figurative language in the novel as

"Ah ain't had a thing on mah stomach today exceptin' mah hand." (4–5)

"Put me down easy Janie, Ah'm a cracked plate." (19)

"Love ain't somethin' lak a grindstone." (182)

In fiction Hurston had the opportunity to proclaim, "I am the product of a tradition where mules go to heaven and buzzards talk," but that is quite different from being identified solely as the reporter of such a tradition, or being identified as the living example of such a tradition for wealthy patrons. Fiction was a way to

44

escape the direct self-consciousness of the interlocutionary moment.

To be limited to *being* the folk creates a situation that will almost certainly end in either frustration, as it did for Hurston during the patronage period of 1925–32, or result in fiction, as it did for Hurston after 1932, when she wrote *Their Eyes Were Watching God.*

As is usual with black artists in America, the personal dimension to such a magnificent work of fiction turns out to be very complicated indeed.

NOTES

1. Cary Nelson, "Introduction," *Theory in the Classroom,* ed. Nelson (Urbana: University of Illinois Press, 1986), p. xiv.
2. Nelson, *Theory in the Classroom,* pp. 3–6.
3. Some anthologies focusing on the Harlem Renaissance include Arna Bontemps, ed., *The Harlem Renaissance Remembered* (New York: Dodd, Mead, and Company, 1972); Nathan Huggins, ed., *Voices from the Harlem Renaissance* (New York: Oxford University Press, 1976); and, more recently, Victor A. Kramer, ed., *The Harlem Renaissance Re-examined* (New York: AMS Press, 1987). The classic anthology of this period remains Alain Locke's seminal collection produced during the Harlem Renaissance, *The New Negro: An Interpretation* (1925. New York: Atheneum, 1968). Recent book-length studies of the period include Houston A. Baker, Jr., *Modernism and the Harlem Renaissance* (Chicago: University of Chicago Press, 1987); Gloria T. Hull, *Color, Sex, and Poetry: Three Women Writers of the Harlem Renaissance* (Bloomington: Indiana University Press, 1987); and Cary Wintz, *Black Culture and the Harlem Renaissance* (Houston: Rice University Press, 1988).
4. Darwin Turner's chapter, "Zora Neale Hurston: The Wandering Minstrel," in his *In a Minor Chord: Three Afro-American Writers and Their Search for Identity* (Carbondale: Southern Illinois University Press, 1971), contains the strongest attack on Hurston. Huggins and Lewis, while also critical, present more balanced accounts of the patronage issue as it relates to Hurston. See Nathan Irvin Huggins, *Harlem Renaissance* (New York: Oxford University Press, 1971), pp. 129–33, and

David Levering Lewis, *When Harlem Was in Vogue* (New York: Alfred A. Knopf, 1981).

5. For an extended discussion of this relationship, see Robert Hemenway, *Zora Neale Hurston: A Literary Biography* (Urbana: University of Illinois Press, 1977), pp. 104–17, 127–33, 138–47, and 175–85.

6. See Zora Neale Hurston, *Dust Tracks on a Road*, ed. Robert Hemenway (1942. Urbana: University of Illinois Press, 1984), pp. 209–12.

7. For another discussion of this issue, see Bruce Kellner, "'Refined Racism': White Patronage in the Harlem Renaissance," in *The Harlem Renaissance Re-examined*, pp. 93–106.

8. For Hughes's discussion of Charlotte Osgood Mason's patronage of his early career, see *The Big Sea* (New York: Hill and Wang, 1940), pp. 312–26.

9. This essay is reprinted in *I Love Myself When I Am Laughing . . . : A Zora Neale Hurston Reader*, ed. Alice Walker (Old Westbury, NY: Feminist Press, 1979), pp. 152–5.

10. Barbara Johnson, "Thresholds of Difference: Structures of Address in Zora Neale Hurston," *A World of Difference* (Baltimore: Johns Hopkins University Press, 1987), pp. 177–8.

11. Henry Louis Gates, Jr., "Criticism in the Jungle," in *Black Literature and Literary Theory*, ed. Gates (New York: Methuen, 1984), p. 6.

12. The field recordings of Hurston's expedition with Lomax and Barnicle are available in the Archive of Folk Song at the Library of Congress (Archive of Folk Song 309-85). What follows in the text is a transcription of part of that recording.

13. Other examples of this interchange between Hurston and Lomax include the following:

Hurston: This one some of them call it "Poor Boy" and some of them call it "Poor Gal," but it is a pretty well distributed blues tune all over the South. The words are not rhymed. It's the typical Negro pattern of the same line repeated three times with a sort of flip line on the end and the change is in the tune rather than in the words for the most part.

Lomax: Where did you pick up the way you sing it?

Hurston: I've known that all of my life, but I've kept learning verses as I've gone around . . .

Hurston: My name is Zora Neale Hurston. I was born in Eatonville, Florida. I am thirty-five years old. This song I am going to sing is a real old song that I found at a railroad gang near Miami and was sung to me by Mack Ford, an old railroad employee, on a construction gang.

Lomax: How long ago was that?

Hurston: That was in 1930.

Lomax: How did you happen to be going around getting songs?

Hurston: I was collecting folk material for Columbia University, College of Anthropology . . .

Hurston: This song I got in Callahan, Florida which is a railroad center in the northern part of Florida. I got this in 1935. I don't remember the man's name who sung it, but I got it at Callahan, the railroad camp.

Lomax: What kind of song is it?

Hurston: This is a not exactly a song. It's a chant for the men lining. You know a rail weighs 900 pounds and the men have to take lining bars and get in shape to spike it down. And while they are doing that, they have a chant and also some songs that they use the rhythm to work it into place, and then boss hollers "Bring my hammer, gang," and they start to spike it down. And this is a chant for lining the rail.

Lomax: I would like you to do that again, but this time when they have . . . what do they call the irons that they use for?

Hurston: They call them a lining bar.

Lomax: All right. The lining bar, when they work, don't you hear the clink of it?

Hurston: There's just a *"ha."* You don't hear the lining bar because it is under the rail and they shove the rail with it. But you can't hear it. It's a crowbar.

Lomax: Because over in Mississippi they showed me by hitting the thing and they said that the way that they did it was several men taking a short pick.

Hurston: Well, I've seen them take it and put it between their legs this way and put it back and they get the flange under the rail and then they ha, ha.

Lomax: What do they do? Are they pulling it?

Hurston: They are pulling it back; they are moving it backwards.

Lomax: In other words, they have it underneath, and they are using the lever to go forward.

Hurston: Yes.

Lomax: All right.

Hurston: And all the men, because it's awful straining, go "ha."

Lomax: About how many men are there on a bar?

Hurston: Oh, sometimes it's about seven or eight on at one time.

Lomax: Suppose you try and sing it again.

Hurston: All right . . .

New Essays on Their Eyes Were Watching God

Hurston: This song I am going to sing is a lining rhythm and I'm going to call it "Mule on the Mount" but you can start with any verse and give it any name and it's the most widely distributed work song in the United States. It has innumerable verses and what not about anything under the sun, and it's a lining rhythm, though sometimes they sing it just sitting around the juke houses and [not] doing any kind of work at all. Chopping wood in the lumber camps and everywhere you'll find this song, nowhere you can't find parts of this song, "Mule on the Mount."

Lomax: It is a consistent song when you hear it, as you hear it all over?

Hurston: The tune is consistent, but the verses – in every locality you find some new verses, everywhere.

Lomax: I mean, does it have the same core of verses? Does it have "Mule on the Mount" everywhere you hear it?

Hurston: There are some places that I have not heard that same verse "Mule on the Mount," but there is no place that I don't hear some of the same verses.

Lomax: Where did you learn this particular way of singing it?

Hurston: Well, I heard the first verse I got in my native village of Eatonville, Florida, from George Thomas.

Lomax: Is this just the one version you are going to sing?

Hurston: I'm going to sing, the tune is the same, I'm going to sing verses from a whole lots of places . . .

Lomax: When you hear that song, about how many verses would a man do? Not as many [as] you do?

Hurston: Yes, sometimes they sing thirty or forty verses. It's one of these songs that have grown by incremental repetition until it's perhaps the longest song in America . . .

Hurston: "Uncle Bud" is not a work song, it's a sort of social song for amusement and it's so widely distributed, it's growing all of the time by incremental repetition, and it is known all over the South. No matter where you go, you can find verses of Uncle Bud. It's the favorite song, and the men get to working in every kind of work, and they just yell down on Uncle Bud and nobody in particular gets the lead, everybody puts in his verse when he is ready. Uncle Bud goes and goes and goes.

Lomax: Is it sung in front of the respectable ladies?

Hurston: Never! It's one of those juke songs. The woman they sing Uncle Bud in front of is a juke woman.

Lomax: I thought you heard it from women?

Hurston: I heard it from a woman. (laughter)

48

14. Barbara Johnson, "Thresholds of Difference," p. 178.
15. Henry Louis Gates, Jr., *The Signifying Monkey: A Theory of Afro-American Literary Criticism* (New York: Oxford University Press, 1988), p. 201.

3

"Crayon Enlargements of Life": Zora Neale Hurston's *Their Eyes Were Watching God* as Autobiography

NELLIE McKAY

The plot was far from the circumstances, but I tried to embalm all the tenderness of my passion for him in *Their Eyes Were Watching God*.

What Zora took from this relationship was the quality of its emotion; its tenderness, its intensity, and perhaps its sense of ultimate impossibility. . . . The man she was leaving . . . was left hurt and confused, wondering if she was "crying on the inside." She gave him her answer in *Their Eyes Were Watching God*. [1]

1

EVERYONE who knows anything about Zora Neale Hurston knows that *Their Eyes Were Watching God* is not her autobiography. Yet the novel is autobiographical on two levels. First, in a continuation of one of the oldest traditions in fiction, Janie tells us the story of how and why her life came to be in the place that it is; second, we also know that Hurston invested this narrative with the joy and pain of her own experiences of female development and romantic love, familiar conventions in women's narratives. Thus, *Their Eyes Were Watching God* offers an opportunity to examine the autobiographical impulse from the perspectives of author Hurston, the writerly self, and fictional Janie, the speakerly self, creating a common text delineating a black female self-in-writing. In their combined oral and written narrative, Hurston and Janie reinforce Janet Varner Gunn's theory of the autobiographer as self-reader, writing (and speaking) from the "outside in, not inside out — or in other words, from the position of the *other* side of [the] lived past which the reader-self occupies" at the time of writing. In this paradigm, Gunn expands the boundaries of "reader" and "reading" to make the reader not only one of "person," but also of "position," permitting the subject of the text to be the participant-observer par excellence – the main character in, narrator, author, and reader of his/her book-like life; and to make reading an interpretative activity in which "clear and certain knowledge of determinate meanings" gives way to "contingent historical experience" and "richer depth in human significance."[2]

Autobiography as an activity that takes place from the outside in rather than from the inside out returns the debate on the subject to an issue that theorists of the genre disagree on: the nature of the "I" behind the self-in-writing. On one side of the question, the "classical" theorists, representing a dominant mainstream Euro-American perspective, promote the sovereignty of the private "I" as the basis of the genre. They perceive this self, writing outward from the inside, as the best and only source of self-knowledge, knowing itself only in isolation and forever remaining hidden behind its public version. "Unsituated" from the world of its environment, it is the timeless, unchanging, absolute, ineffable self that no one else knows. Language cannot capture such a self, and produces only a mask behind which the true self hides. On the other side of the question, another group of critics, those who study mainly the lives of women and Third World people, argue for the preeminence of a different kind of self in autobiography. They hold that at best the hidden, private "I" represents a privileged group, mostly white and male. They promote the existence of an inclusive "I" that places the autobiographer inside of and inseparable from the cultural context which, they say, informs his or her identity. From this perspective, autobiography, Gunn suggests, is not the mask that hides the true self, but the revelation of an unalienated, *displayed* or representative self joined to the world through an understanding of shared humanity. Instead of "the private act of a self writing, autobiography becomes the cultural act of a self reading" against the background of time, place, race, class, gender, and the other variables that define individual members of particular groups.[3] In other words, the written self evolves as one that has a past, a present, and a future in relationship to others, and the autobiographer develops his or her identity within the cultural contours of the peculiar environment that shaped the self.

From the beginning, scholars of Afro-American autobiography have been in general agreement on the extent to which social and cultural forces influence Afro-American identity. Textual evidence shows that, in the face of various oppressions, the black self achieves a wholesome identity through awareness and acceptance of interdependence between the individual and his or her support-ive community and the knowledge that collective black American physical and psychological survival depends on the union (even when troubled) of the individual and the group. In this respect, the Afro-American autobiographer writes not from an internal posi-tion of isolated selfhood, but from having to interpret, to read the self, if you will (as writer and reader of the text), through preexist-ing layers of group social acculturation that empower and shape that individual self. *Their Eyes Were Watching God,* Janie's story, simultaneously written and told, emerges as a composite "read-ing" of black female growth and development against the history of the oppression of race and sex. This narrative reinforces the cultural approach to identity that has dominated the Afro-American male-centered tradition from the slave narratives of the nineteenth century to the present time, but it also makes of the "autobiographical situation" another vehicle for the self-em-powerment of black women.

2

The epigraphs that begin this essay – Zora Neale Hurston's auto-biographical call to her text, and Robert Hemenway's biographical response to her voice – illustrate an act of cultural significance that implicitly informs and illuminates the nature of the Afro-American autobiographical impulse in *Their Eyes Were Watching God.* In his sympathetic reading of the space in which the author and her narrative meet, Hemenway affirms Hurston's ability to translate the passions of her lived experiences into poignant creative achievement through fictional autobiography told in multiple voices. Furthermore, these voices assure us that both narrator and character "read" these experiences against the background of the history of black women's realities in America. The circumstances of the autobiography and the fiction were indeed different, but writer Hurston – the experiencing self – and character Janie – the narrative self – take us on a journey of personal discovery to the place where language, gender, and culture merge to give full voice to the otherwise often-marginalized black female self. In fact, the feeling woman embedded the kind of emotional tenderness into the novel that makes it a model of what Bella Brodzki and Celeste Schenck call "the duplicitous and complicitous relationship of 'life' and 'art' in autobiographical modes."[4] In the Hurston text, the image of actual and fictional self spreads across a large canvas that challenges conventional female identity and the representative autobiographical self of the male canon. Returned from burying the figurative and literal dead of their discourses, writer and character share common ground in the unfolding of their story: Janie's autobiography, Hurston's metaphor. In the mingling of their complementary voices reading themselves into the canon, Hurston gains immortality in the literary tradition, whereas Janie inserts her voice into the Afro-American oral tradition.

In Afro-American literature, fiction and autobiography share a long history of common boundaries. Although few would dispute the claim that autobiography has been the preeminent form of writing among blacks for more than 150 years, all agree that this genre influences and is influenced by fiction, a reciprocal relationship that forces each to greater experimentation. For instance, from its earliest beginnings, by adopting the artfulness and rhetorical structures more usually identified with fiction, black autobiography made of itself a form that signified as well as signified on the totality of the Afro-American experience. Subsequently, complementing each other over time, both have, to their greater advantage, shared similar expressive strategies. As a result, contemporary Afro-American autobiographers are among avant-garde writers in the genre who constantly transgress the narrative boundaries of fiction and autobiography. Thus, in appraising Afro-American traditions in narrative, readers face difficulties when they attempt to separate life and art, nature and imitation, autobiography and fiction.[5] Hurston and later black women writers have taken full advantage of the flexibility of this tradition.[6]

"Crayon Enlargements of Life" explores autobiographical themes in *Their Eyes Were Watching God* as the personal narrative of Janie Crawford Killicks Starks Woods, acknowledging the location of some of its major points of reference in the life of Zora Neale Hurston. Hurston's reputation rests on her work as one of the most important literary figures to emerge from the Harlem Renaissance of the 1920s; she is best known as a champion of the primacy of black folk culture, and for her challenge to conventional social expectations of female conduct in relationships between men and women. As a writer in the twentieth century, she was among the early black women unequivocally to assert women's rights to self-fulfillment outside of their allegiances to men. Within a framework that recognizes the significance of black folk life to the psychological health of black people, and women's right to autonomy, this essay addresses (1) Hurston's delineation of Janie's psychological journey from a male-identified female to assertive womanhood; (2) her exploration of self-acceptance and black identity in a response to such a work as James Weldon Johnson's *The Autobiography of An Ex-Coloured Man;*[7] (3) Janie's text as a vehicle that restores black voice to the as-told-to slave narratives of the nineteenth century; and (4) Janie's achievement of voice. In the combination of these themes, *Their Eyes Were Watching God* is a representative text in the Afro-American cultural tradition, but one that claims a central place for black women. Writ large, Janie's story reflects efforts by black women, writing and speaking their lives, to liberate themselves and all black people from the oppression of race and sex through the power of language and the struggle to own their history.

In spite of general agreement about Afro-American autobiography that locates the black self within the racial community, in their personal successes, male autobiographers much more than their female counterparts credit their successes to individual initiative and personal efforts. On the other hand, black women writing of their lives usually see their gains as a result of the support they receive from others with whom they are associated, especially of other women. Hurston's novel goes further than most to reinforce the role of community in this text, which, as Barbara Christian, among others, has observed, is made strikingly clear in the structure of the work. In the mechanism of the story within a story, author Hurston, the critic notes, presented her heroine "not [as] an individual in a vacuum; . . . [but as] an intrinsic part of a community, [to which she] brings her life and its richness, joys, and sorrows."[8] *Their Eyes Were Watching God* is told partly in standard English by a formal omniscient narrator, who is spectator to and participant in the action; and partly in the intimate voice (black dialect) of its protagonist reflecting on her experiences in the presence of a second-person character – the heroine's closest friend, Pheoby, who also speaks in folk language in her own voice, and to whom Janie entrusts her tale.[9]

Further contributing to this understanding of the cultural interconnectedness between Janie's life and her community, Elizabeth Meese finds that Hurston's "method displays a keen awareness of the performative quality . . . that emerges from the tradition of oral narrative, as well as a clever consciousness of the storyteller-writer's role in constructing the history of a people through language." She also observes that the structure of the story, especially considering the role of Janie's friend as chorus/audience, enables Hurston to draw more fully on the "rich oral legacy of black female storytelling and mythmaking that has its roots in Afro-American culture." The writer's aim, Meese points out, is to transform the separate texts within her text into an integrated text; that is, she melds Janie's orality and the narrator's intertexts into a unitary self-contained text that symbolizes "a form of feminist self-definition."[10] The Janie who emerges in this newly formed text represents a harmonious interrelationship among writer, storyteller, and community, as Hurston and Janie, in unfolding Janie's story, change the private autobiographical act into a search for a collective black self that does not negate the importance of her separate parts. The success of this work rests on the harmony of its multiple voices telling stories individually or in dialogue with one another.

None of these other voices diminish the significance of the final rendering of Janie's voice that emerges from the community she helps to form, and which also forms her. Still, her voice does not dominate the narrative space. The third-person narrator participates and shares in similar communal activities as Janie: selecting, shaping, and presenting portions of the unfolding story. Thus, she also functions as a source to bring the reader into closer contact with the community. Within this arrangement, as John Callahan notes, writer Hurston exists alongside of Janie, not in front of or behind her. In sharing the same space, the two are like composer and performer in a drama that celebrates black life.[11] The success of their collective storytelling is in the ability that it gives Janie to take control of the "pulpit" from which she finally speaks and fulfills her grandmother's aborted desire to "preach a great sermon about colored women sittin' on high" (15). The granddaughter's sermon is one that the grandmother could never have imagined, for Janie's narrative bears testimony, not from a seat on high, but out of the matrix of the strength of black women who, for generations, in Toni Morrison's words, were both ship and safe harbor in their communities, but who, often at great cost to themselves, refused to be the mules of the world.

As a professional anthropologist and an Afro-American with deep roots in the cultural life of the folk, Hurston's choice of narrative mode reflects conscious intentions to preserve intrinsic folk forms and values as a vital part of the Afro-American personal identity. But she did not think that in order to be part of the group, one was compelled to sacrifice individuality and freedom from intragroup oppression. As she did in her own life, she permitted her heroine the independence to make decisions, achieve voice, and speak her life as an individual distinct from her community. Still, in relinquishing proprietary claims to the conventional personal narrative, the "I" of *Their Eyes Were Watching God* projects a sustaining connection to the roots of black culture through which her development occurs.

3

As autobiography, *Their Eyes Were Watching God* is an important text in the literature of the quest for freedom and self. In American life and writing, as experience and metaphor, white and black women have a long history of the journey as a vital part of their traditions. Among the former, the letters, diaries, and journals of pioneer women traveling with their families from east to west provide one of our most useful sources of information on life situations in the settling of the country. In the tradition of Afro-American autobiography, beginning with the slave and spiritual narratives, traveling, physically and psychologically, in search of self and freedom was an intimate part of the lives of Afro-American women and men. For early black women writers, travel and journey became an activity closely associated with the freedom to choose useful and dignified lives. Excluding the slave and spiritual narratives, a large body of nineteenth- and twentieth-century travel writings by black women exist: the stories of women like Nancy Prince, *A Narrative of the Life and Travels of Mrs. Prince* (1856), Mary Church Terrell, *A Colored Woman in a White World* (1940), Era Bell Thompson, *Africa: Land of My Fathers* (1954), and Charlotte Crogman Wright, *Beneath the Southern Cross: The Story of an American Bishop's Wife in South Africa* (1955), to name a few. In spite of the racial, sexual, and economic oppression they encountered on their journeys, the authors of these texts used their travel experiences to explore various aspects of black women's realities. Writing as a tool of self-discovery and self-revelation enabled them to declare their commitment to action and social change, to express their sense of personal and group empowerment, to clarify their engagement with the world and their willingness to take responsibility for the decisions and actions that affected their lives. Travel writings also permitted the handing down of individual acts of personal heroism as examples for future generations.

Janie's text is another link in the chain of black women's travel stories in the quest for self. Her conscious journey is of major importance for her psychological development from a male-identified woman to a self firmly grounded in a positive sense of independent black womanhood. This search begins for her in northern Florida when she is sixteen, in her "awakening" "beneath the pear tree soaking in the alto chant of visiting bees" (10), and ends with her return to Eatonville after a stay of eighteen months on the muck of the Everglades. The narrative takes place in more than twenty years through deep and meaningful changes in her life. By the end, her story reflects the quality of self-discovery, self-empowerment, and personal heroism that is the hallmark of the tradition that it enters.

The first leg of her journey, of which Janie is unconscious of its meaning, occurs when she is a young child. This segment takes her from the servants' quarters in "de white folks yard" to her grandmother's house on a small plot of land, secured through hard work and sacrifice on the older woman's part. This was Nanny's attempt to enable the child to grow up with a sense of worth, independent of white people. But if the move invests Janie with the dignity of racial pride, by the time she reaches the first blush of womanhood she discovers the restrictive bonds of woman's place in man's world, qualitatively as soul-destroying as the experiences of racism. But Nanny, who suffered the worst of black female sexual oppression, first as a slave, and later in the knowledge of the rape of her only child (Janie's mother), does not understand this. Instead, she encircles Janie with a love that ushers her into the prisonhouse of the male-identified woman, a condition that confines women from their own lives. Nanny's justification of the young girl's marriage to the aging but financially secure Logan Killicks for safety and protection from other men condones the patriarchal oppression of women. Discrediting the merits of romantic love and personal growth as the "prong all us black women gits hung on," her ethic subscribes to the maintenance of male dominance over women's lives (22). That Logan has the authority, and even is expected to abuse Janie physically, does not disturb the old woman. Her lifelong pain and suffering as an unprotected black woman lead Nanny to wish for the assurance of a secure marriage for Janie before she (Nanny) dies. Her unawareness of the politics of gender roles convinces her that, safely married, "maybe de menfolks white or black [will not make] a spit cup outa [Janie]." Pleading for understanding, she implores: "Put me down easy, Janie," "Ah'm a cracked plate" (19).

The moves from the white folks' yard to Nanny's house, and subsequently to that of Logan Killicks, were involuntary on Janie's part. Not so the journey away from Logan's "lonesome place [which looked to Janie] like a stump in the middle of the woods" (20). Unknown to her, that move was in the making even before she knew she was to marry Killicks. The initial steps occurred on that spring afternoon when the chant of kissing bees in the blossoming pear tree awakened her to the mystery of life and nature. The hum that reached her was "like a flute song forgotten in another existence and remembered again" (10). At the time, surrendering herself to her instincts, she yearned to be a pear tree, or any other tree in bloom, with "glossy leaves and bursting buds, and she wanted to struggle with life" (23, 25). Logan Killicks, no singing bee to her blossom, merely desecrated that vision of herself. Later, unimpressed by his paid-for house and sixty acres of land, or her new status as the only black woman in town to own an organ, when he threatened to assert his authority by declaring that she work the mule and plow in his potato field, after initial hesitation, she walked away with Joe Starks. The step was a risk. Joe did not "represent sun-up and pollen and blooming trees," nor did he make speeches to her "with rhymes," but he spoke of far horizons, bought her generous gifts, and said he wanted her with him when he became a "big voice."

Although the men were different, twenty years of life as Joe's wife proved equally as confining for Janie as her shorter time with Logan Killicks. Logan saw his identity reflected in the success and respect that came to him through hard work, ownership of property, and possession of a young and pretty wife. Joe's god was the lust for power and control over the whole community, including his wife. Janie asserted her individuality by refusing to conform to her husbands' dreams of her, and holding on to her dream of a loving partnership that recognized true equity between each member of the marriage team.

"There are years that ask questions and years that answer [them]," Hurston tells us of Janie's development (20). Before she married Killicks, she had little time to frame the significant questions of the future that stretched before her, and none to learn the answers in. "Did marriage end the cosmic loneliness of the un-mated? Did marriage compel love like the sun the day?" By the time she left him, however, she knew that marriage did not make love, and in this death of her first dream, Hurston remarks, Janie became a woman. In the years of her marriage to Joe, she learned other answers. For a time the struggle between them was keen. He wanted her submission, she would not give in and struggled against him. After a while, "the spirit of the marriage left the bedroom and took to living in the parlor . . . to shake hands whenever company came to visit" (67). What followed were years of profound psychological growth for Janie. She discovered that she had an inside and an outside and that she could keep them separate from each other. She knew that the Joe she had run off with had been a youthful illusion – not the "flesh and blood figure of her dreams . . . [but] something she had grabbed up to drape her dreams over" (68). Buried deep inside her, she packed and stored away the thoughts and emotions she never expressed to him. In time, she hoped to find someone to share them with. Meanwhile, she had two lives. In one she carried out her wifely tasks and as much as possible avoided confrontations with Joe. In the other, she developed a self hidden from everyone else.

> One day she sat and watched the shadow of herself going about tending store and prostrating itself before Joe, while all the time she herself sat under a shady tree with the wind blowing through her hair and her clothes. . . . After awhile it [this vision] got so common she ceased to be surprised by it. . . . it reconciled her to things. (119)

So complete was her ability to keep her selves apart from each other that when Joe died she sent her public face to the funeral while her private self "went rollicking with the springtime across the world" (137).

Hurston scholars disagree on the extent of Tea Cake's contributions to the subsequent full emergence of Janie's voice and self. That he was instrumental in showing her the possibilities of a life outside of materialistic and social restrictions, one built instead on honest love and respect between people, is not in dispute. But Janie had spent the greater part of her second marriage in a journey seeking her selfhood. By the time Tea Cake came into her life she was ready to embrace life willingly and fully. Her awakening under the blossoming pear tree at age sixteen was a call to "journey to the horizon in search of *people*" (85). Instead, her grandmother had sent her on a path "down a back road after *things*" (85). She found those things: financial stability and social position, with Logan Killicks and Joe Starks, but they never satisfied her. Tea

Cake showed her how to give herself in love and to reach out to others in acceptance of their love.

When Nanny insisted that Janie marry Logan Killicks, she questioned neither the price that women paid for male protection nor the implications of the other's ownership of women's bodies and their wills. She never admitted alternatives to women's subservience to men. Although she meant well where Janie was concerned, the extent of her own victimization by race and sex made of her intentions what Janie called "mis-love." For, out of ignorance, Nanny "had taken the biggest thing God ever made, the horizon . . . and pinched it in to such a little bit of a thing that she could tie it about her granddaughter's neck tight enough to choke her" (85). First, in her literal abandonment of Logan Killicks, and later in her psychological separation from Joe, Janie rejects her grandmother's misguided vision of black women's lives in favor of the journey to the horizon in search of the independent self.

Unlike many other protagonists in black women's autobiographical narratives, Janie has no female models, no mother or female relatives from whose examples she learns to pattern her acts of rebellion against the peculiar oppressions that confront all black women. However, in the relationship between Janie and Pheoby, especially after Janie's return from the muck – Pheoby's act of bringing food to her friends, Janie's recitation of her story to Pheoby, the latter's response to the story, and Janie's investiture of Pheoby with the authority to communicate the story to the women in the community – the narrative affirms the significance of female bonding in women's search for their identities. In spite of their initial jealousy, the attitudes of the women of Eatonville will change toward Janie when they discover the person she has become. Freed from the yoke of the title of Mrs. Mayor, and secure in her identity as one of them, she will participate in the community rituals from which her social position had previously excluded her. Her life will shape theirs as much as theirs will continue to shape hers.

In narratives of quest, ex-slave women wrote of the hardships they endured in slavery and during the hazardous journeys they took in search of physical and psychological freedom. Free black women used travel stories to emphasize their efforts toward greater control over their lives. Always, travel insinuated quest for self by rejecting boundaries and limitations on the self.

Janie characterizes her journey as the trip to "de big 'ssociation of life . . . De Grand Lodge, de big convention of livin" (6). She traveled to the horizon of her own dreams, and in this place of personal fulfillment we leave her ready to settle down to help to enrich the life of her community. In choosing love and equal partnership over financial security and materialistic concerns, she takes a bold step toward the emotional health that had not previously been hers. The relationship with Tea Cake helped to shape her self-knowledge, but in his death she is free to discover security in herself, and the courage to speak in her own black woman's voice, no longer dependent on men. Claiming the joys and pains of all her experiences as components of her identity, Janie finally comes to the end of the journey begun under the blossoming pear tree more than twenty years before. She had been to the horizon. Now she would begin to live through her newly found woman-identified self.

In addition to the successful journey from male-identified to self-identified woman, Janie's positive black self-concept at the end of her narrative can be read as Hurston's response to anxieties of identity common among black people in her time. From the end of the nineteenth century through the early part of the twentieth, many Afro-Americans, especially those who aspired to middle-class status and privilege, were especially frustrated by the oppressiveness of marginality as members of a group labeled inferior. During this period, the prevalence of novels and autobiographical accounts of the phenomenon of passing was one indication of the magnitude of this anxiety. In the most drastic measure against these feelings, a number of those who could, by means of their physical appearances, rejected their black identity and passed into the white world. Janie's story, set almost exclusively inside of the black community, embodies none of the overt conventions of passing, yet inversely addresses anxieties of racial identity. The stories are different, but Janie's text, read against that of the ex-colored man in James Weldon Johnson's novel for instance, is a good example of Hurston's rejection of black self-hate implicit in passing or other destructive behaviors associated with internalization of a negative black racial identity.

Janie's achievement of positive identification with the black community is in stark contrast to the failure of the protagonist of Johnson's novel to admit kinship with the group. His final alienation from Afro-America is as fixed as her connectedness to it. Interestingly, both characters begin their lives unaware of their racial identities, and as children, both undergo epiphanies that transform their innocence into profound knowledge. Each child reacts differently to the situation in which he or she discovers blackness. As a young boy, Johnson's questing antihero never thinks about race because he has no reason to believe that he is other than white until an insensitive white school teacher informs him otherwise. Psychologically diminished by this revelation, in a scene reminiscent of one involving Valet de Chambre in Mark Twain's *Pudd'nhead Wilson,* amidst a flood of tears, he inquires of his mulatto mother: "Tell me . . . am I a nigger?"[12] From the moment that he discovers his "tainted" blood, he lives with ambivalence toward his racial self. Ultimately, he passes for white and becomes an ex-colored man.

Janie's awakening is different. She discovers her racial self out of her inability to recognize her image in a photograph in which she appears among a group of white playmates. However, her identity is further fragmented by the fact that because many people have named her differently, she is called Alphabet. She, like the ex-colored man, receives the vital information from a white adult. Surprised but not traumatized by it, she looks at the photograph more closely until she recognizes herself by her clothes and hair. But unlike the ex-colored man, who feels great shame, when confronted with this information, Janie accepts herself fully. For Johnson's character, the knowledge is the dread discovery of the self as "nigger"; for her, it is the truth of who she is. She responds in surprise, not pain: "Aw, aw! Ah'm colored!" For him, the discovery represents expulsion from a community of choice.

Janie and the orphaned ex-colored man, equally unworldly, set out in their youth to find themselves as individuals and to establish their places within communities. At the conclusion of his narrative self, the protagonist of Johnson's text, now a successful "white"

businessman in his middle years, acknowledges with some regret
that through the life choices he made, he exchanged the integrity
of his racial birthright for the psychic emptiness of materialism and
social safety in a white world that did not know his true identity.
When he takes psychological stock of his social and economic
gains from the exchange, he tries to convince himself that his
action links him directly to the Afro-American trickster figure –
that paragon of "puttin' on ole master." However, he knows that,
weighted in the balance, even by his own standards, he is wanting.
Not only did he, in cowardly fashion, turn his back on the world of
his mother's people, but in his retreat from the reality of self, he
squandered his great musical talents through which he could have
made a major contribution to the enhancement and preservation
of the culture of his group. His future holds prospects of painful
regrets hidden in his dark secret.

One of the important advantages of his passing is the financial
security the ex-colored man is able to establish for himself and his
children. By the end of the narrative, he is a wealthy man with
leisure time to contemplate his life. Although he is stoic in his
acceptance of responsibility for the emotional barrenness his self-
rejection creates for him, the psychological cost is high. His secret
may never be revealed, but as he rightly surmises, like the Biblical
Esau, he sold his birthright for a mess of pottage.

On the other hand, Janie rejects the soul-limiting options of
materialism and social safety twice in her life – once when she
walks away from Logan Killicks's sixty acres, two mules, and an
organ in the parlor, and a second time when, after Joe's death, she
agrees to marry Tea Cake rather than one of her more affluent
suitors. At the end of the novel, as she places her experiences in
their proper places in her development, she has no regrets, for
even her mistakes have helped to shape her. She sees "her life like
a great tree in leaf with the things suffered, things enjoyed, things
done, and undone. Dawn and doom was in its branches" (8). She
accepts all of the parts as contributions to the wholesome black
female self whom she embraces.

In his study of the search for voice in twentieth-century African-
American literature, John F. Callahan observes that the distinct
voices in Hurston's novel represent the Afro-American call-and-

response dialogue that originated in the oral culture. While Callahan focuses his discussion of narrative form on the author's independent stand against certain modernist trends in literature, and her call to readers to "respond to Janie Crawford's story . . . with 'new thought' and 'new words'" (116), it is also a text that looks backward to nineteenth-century autobiographical narrative.

Their Eyes Were Watching God bears a close resemblance to the traditional as-told-to slave narrative of the earlier period, but in the safety of the noncompeting voices that tell and write the story, it revises the former by returning voice (in the language of the untutored) to the silenced ex-slave of previous times. In these nineteenth-century narratives, the call of the Afro-American "I" elicited, not the harmony of a comprehending Afro-American response, but, regardless of his or her sympathy, the dissonance of the white amanuensis-editor who "cropped and framed" the ex-slave's story "according to the standards of an alienating culture." Even when an editor might well have produced the facts of the ex-slave's life, in granting permission to have his or her story rendered in written form by any white editor, the escaped slave lost control of the narrative, and therefore of his or her voice. Conversely, those who gained control of such narratives "assumed the right to do everything [to them] . . . from improving . . . grammar, style, and diction to selecting, arranging, and assigning significance to . . . factual substance."[13]

Janie is not illiterate, but she does not possess the literary skills to render her story in writing. Nor would her intended audiences (Pheoby and the community) have access to that story outside of its oral rendering. In choosing to "speak" her *auto* and *bio* in her own voice, in a language that enables her to communicate directly with her close friend, and by extension the entire folk community, she remains grounded in the culture of her people and speaks for those who, having no options, once told their stories to white people who deprived them of narrative authority and compromised the authenticity of their documents. Unlike them, she puts her voice into the mouth of her friend. She can also confidently entrust the integrity of the *graphe* of her discourse to the black female narrator who responds responsibly to the "call" as she writes Janie's text into the literate culture. This collaborator-narrator, unlike the nineteenth-century white editor, comments and elaborates on Janie's text but does not "edit" the heroine out of her story. Important examples of this reciprocality of voice and speech can be noted in Hurston's meticulous care to avoid hierarchical privileging of either the oral or written discourse in the similarity of the storyteller's and the narrator's use of metaphor, in the function of black folk colloquialisms and diction, and in the ways in which narrator and character manufacture words for special effects. Such a convergence of the two aspects of language was impossible to achieve in the collaboration between escaped slave and nineteenth-century white editor.

In fact, at all levels, in the search for language through which to make themselves heard, black slave narrators felt disjunction in their relationships with sympathetic whites. Those who were literate, and who wrote their own stories, experienced great anxieties over their perceived inadequacy with the written word to express fully their emotional responses to slavery. This anxiety was only increased by the dilemma of the ex-slave's uncertainty of whether the whites who championed his or her cause really wanted to know the truth of those feelings.[14] In Hurston's novel, Janie tells her story to her friend who, in turn, will repeat that story to the community in the language they share. Even in the double transference (Pheoby's retelling and the narrator's writing) Janie's voice remains the most vital instrument in her story. To borrow from Houston A. Baker, Jr., that voice is one of "lyrical, autobiographical recall . . . [Janie is] a singer who . . . recapitulates the blues experience of all black women."[15]

A significant aspect of the control that both Nanny and Joe Starks impose on Janie is silence, about which much has been written. But silence also creates loneliness for her, as the social status that comes to her through the affluence and authority of her first two husbands separates her from the community of women. Both "class" her off, and successfully separate her from the other women. Still, even when she acquiesces to their demands on her, internally, Janie rejects and struggles against the emptiness and loneliness of the positions they would have her fill.

Janie's meeting with Tea Cake, who fulfills the role of the bee to her blossom, opens the way for her to construct a language of liberation through what Elizabeth Meese calls the "discourse of emotion." With Tea Cake, she tells Pheoby, "new thoughts had tuh be thought and new words said. . . . He done taught me the maiden language all over."[16] The new language she appropriates not only facilitates her relationship with Tea Cake, but also permits her to join the communities from which she was previously excluded, first on the muck and then in Eatonville. With this language she can engage in telling big stories, even as she had only listened to them before, she can reject Mrs. Turner's ideas of the hierarchy of color, and she develops her own text on class and sex.

The autobiographical "I" in *Their Eyes Were Watching God* finds self and voice in forging a new history constructed out of the handing down of one woman's story of liberation to another. Exchanging outsideness for individuality within the community, Janie becomes a feminist heroine with an assured place within that community, and her life becomes an influential source through which other women will find a model for their own self-empowerment. Pheoby will not be the only one to grow ten feet taller or be dissatisfied with herself on hearing Janie's story. For the first time in her life, Janie can celebrate herself through what she learns in the call and response of a relationship of shared love, intimacy, and autonomy. Her voice constitutes a force for liberation within the community of women.

Unlike the solitary but representative hero of male autobiography, Janie Starks and Zora Neale Hurston join voices to produce a personal narrative that celebrates an individual and collective black female identity emerging out of the search for an autonomous self. Although the structure of this text is different, the tradition of black women celebrating themselves through other women like themselves began with their personal narratives of the nineteenth century. Female slave narratives, we know, generally had protagonists who shared their space with the women who instilled pride of self and love of freedom in them. The tradition continued into the twentieth century. For instance, much of the early portion of Hurston's autobiography, *Dust Tracks on a Road*, celebrates the relationship she had with her mother and the lessons she learned, directly and indirectly, from other women in the community. Thus,

"Crayon Enlargements of Life"

Hurston's structure for Janie's story expands that already existing tradition to concretize the symbolic rendering of voice to and out of the women's community by breaking away from the formalities of conventional autobiography to make Janie's text an autobiography about autobiographical storytelling,[17] in the tradition of African and Afro-American storytelling. Hurston, struggling with the pains and ambivalences she felt toward the realities of a love she had to reject for the restraints it would have placed on her, found a safe place to embalm the tenderness and passion of her feelings in the autobiographical voice of Janie Crawford, whose life she made into a very fine crayon enlargement of life.

NOTES

1. Zora Neale Hurston, *Dust Tracks on a Road*, ed. Robert Hemenway (1942. Reprint: Urbana: University of Illinois Press, 1984), p. 260; Robert Hemenway, *Zora Neale Hurston: A Literary Biography* (Urbana: University of Illinois Press, 1978), p. 231.
2. Janet Varner Gunn, *Autobiography: Toward a Poetics of Experience* (Philadelphia: University of Pennsylvania Press, 1982), pp. 6, 12.
3. Gunn, *Autobiography*, p. 8.
4. Bella Brodzki and Celeste Schenck, eds., *Life/Lines – Theorizing Women's Autobiography* (Ithaca: Cornell University Press, 1988), pp. 12–13.
5. Nancy K. Miller, "Writing Fictions: Women's Autobiography in France," in *Life/Lines*, p. 45.
6. For example, the tradition includes Paule Marshall's *Brown Girl, Brownstones*, Alice Walker's *Meridian*, and Louise Meriwether's *Daddy Was a Number Runner*, fictions that are extensively autobiographical.
7. James Weldon Johnson, *The Autobiography of an Ex-Coloured Man* (1912. Reprint: New York: Hill and Wang, 1960).
8. Barbara Christian, *Black Women Novelists: The Development of a Tradition, 1892–1976* (Westport, CT: Greenwood Press, 1980), p. 57.
9. John D. Kalb, "The Anthropological Narrator in Hurston's *Their Eyes Were Watching God*," *Studies in American Fiction* 16 (Autumn 1988): 170.
10. Elizabeth Meese, "Orality and Textuality in *Their Eyes Were Watching God*," in *Modern Critical Interpretations: "Their Eyes Were Watching God*," ed. Harold Bloom (New York: Chelsea House, 1987), p. 61.

69

11. John Callahan, *In the African-American Grain: The Pursuit of Voice in Twentieth-Century Black Fiction* (Urbana: University of Illinois Press, 1988), pp. 125, 127.

12. Johnson, *Ex-Coloured Man*, p. 18.

13. William L. Andrews, *To Tell a Free Story: The First One Hundred Years of Afro-American Autobiography* (Urbana: University of Illinois Press, 1986), p. 38.

14. Andrews, *To Tell a Free Story*, p. 9.

15. Houston A. Baker, Jr., *Blues, Ideology, and Afro-American Literature* (Chicago: University of Chicago Press, 1984), p. 58.

16. Meese, "Orality," p. 173.

17. Sidonie Smith, *A Poetics of Women's Autobiography* (Bloomington: Indiana University Press, 1987), p. 150.

4

The Politics of Fiction, Anthropology, and the Folk: Zora Neale Hurston

HAZEL V. CARBY

THE work of Zora Neale Hurston, in particular the novel *Their Eyes Were Watching God*, has been the object of more than a decade of critical attention. But, in addition to the critical consideration of Hurston's writings, her work has received the level of institutional support necessary for Hurston to enter the American literary mainstream. Two examples of this support would be the special Hurston seminar held at the Modern Language Association annual conference in 1975 and the award of two grants from the National Endowment for the Humanities to Robert Hemenway to write Hurston's biography. Hurston's work has also received institutional support from publishers: The rights to reprint *Their Eyes Were Watching God* in a paperback edition were leased to the University of Illinois Press by Harper and Row, but the 1978 Illinois edition has been so profitable that Harper and Row refused to renew leasing contracts and is reprinting *Their Eyes, Jonah's Gourd Vine, Mules and Men,* and *Tell My Horse* themselves with Henry Louis Gates as series editor. During the years between Hemenway's biography and the new Harper and Row/Gates monopoly of Hurston, there have been a variety of anthologies and collections of Hurston's essays and short stories, and in 1984, a second edition of Hurston's autobiography, *Dust Tracks on a Road,* was published.[1]

As academics we are well aware that we work within institutions that police the boundaries of cultural acceptability and define what is and what is not "literature": Our work as teachers and as critics creates, maintains, and sometimes challenges boundaries of acceptability. Graduate students tell me that they teach *Their Eyes*

Were Watching God at least once a semester; it is a text that is common to a wide variety of courses in African-American Studies, American Studies, English, or Women's Studies. It is frequently the case that undergraduates in the Humanities may be taught the novel as many as four times, or at least once a year during their undergraduate careers. Traditions, of course, are temporal, and are constantly being fought over and renegotiated. Clearly, a womanist- and feminist-inspired desire to recover the neglected cultural presence of Zora Neale Hurston initiated an interest in her work, but it is also clear that this original motivation has become transformed. Hurston is not only a secured presence in the academy; she is a veritable industry, and an industry that is very profitable. The new Harper and Row edition of *Their Eyes* sold its total print run of 75,000 in less than a month.[2] The *New York Times* of February 4, 1990, published an article on Hurston called "Renaissance for a Pioneer of Black Pride" in which it was announced that a play based on Hurston's life and entitled "Zora Neale Hurston: A Theatrical Biography" was opening in New York, and that another play, "Mule Bone," a collaboration with Langston Hughes, is scheduled to open this summer.[3] On February 14, 1990, the Public Broadcasting System, in their prestigious American Playhouse series, broadcast "Zora is My Name" starring Ruby Dee in a dramatization of selections from *Mules and Men* and *Dust Tracks*. Although it could be said that Hurston has "arrived" as a contemporary, national, cultural presence, I await one further development: the announcement of a Hollywood movie.

I am as interested in the contemporary cultural process of the inclusion of Hurston into the academy as I am interested in her writing. I wonder about the relation between the cultural meanings of her work in the 1920s and 1930s and the contemporary fascination with Hurston. How is she being reread, now, to produce cultural meanings that this society wants or needs to hear? Is there, indeed, an affinity between the two discrete histories of her work? Certainly, I can see parallels between the situation of black intellectuals in the 1920s and 1930s, described now as a "Renaissance," and the concerns of black humanists in the academy in the 1980s. Literary histories could doubtless be written about a "renaissance" of black intellectual productivity within the walls of the academy in the post–civil rights era of the twentieth century.

Their Eyes Were Watching God now, of course, has a cultural existence outside of the realm of African-American Studies and independent of scholars of the field, but how tenuous is this presence? Does the current fascination of the culture industry for the cultural production of black women parallel the white fascination for African-American peoples as representatives of the exotic and primitive in the 1920s?[4] And will the current thirst for the cultural production of black women evaporate as easily? Will the economic crisis of the late 1980s and early 1990s be used, in a future literary history, to mark the demise of the black intellectual presence in the academy in the same way as the 1929 stock market crash has been used by literary historians to mark the death of the Harlem Renaissance? If there is a fragile presence of black peoples in universities, is our cultural presence secure or only temporarily profitable? With or without reference to our contemporary economic conditions, it is startlingly obvious that current college enrollment figures reveal a sharp fall in the numbers of black graduate students, figures which would seem to confirm the tenuous nature of our critical presence. But what I find most intriguing is the relation between a crisis of representation that shaped cultural responses to black urban migration after World War I and the contemporary crisis of representation in African-American humanist intellectual work that determines our cultural and critical responses, or the lack of response, to the contemporary crisis of black urban America.[5]

However, let me make a theoretical intervention here. Edward Said has asserted that it is "now almost impossible . . . to remember a time when people were *not* talking about a crisis in representation," and he points to the enormous difficulties of uncertainty and undecidability that are a consequence of transformations "in our notions of formerly stable things such as authors, texts and objects."[6] In an attempt to be as specific as I can about the particular crisis of representation in black cultural production out of which, I am going to argue, Hurston's work emerges, I will try to define some terms.

The subaltern group that is the subject of Hurston's anthropological and fictional work is represented as the rural black
folk. However, the process of defining and representing a subaltern
group is always a contentious issue, and is at the heart of the crisis
of representation in black intellectual thought in both historical
moments.[7] The dominant way of reading the cultural production
of what is called the Harlem Renaissance is that black intellectuals
assertively established a folk heritage as the source of, and inspiration for, authentic African-American art forms. In African-
American studies the Harlem Renaissance has become a convention particularly for literary critics, but it is, as is the case with all
literary histories, an imagined or created historical perspective that
privileges some cultural developments while rendering other cultural and political histories invisible. The dominance of this particular literary history in our work, as opposed to organizing a history around a Chicago Renaissance, for example, has uncritically
reproduced at the center of its discourse the issue of an authentic
folk heritage. The desire of the Harlem intellectuals to establish
and re-present African-American cultural authenticity to a predominantly white audience was a mark of a change from, and
confrontation with, what were seen by them to be externally im-
posed cultural representations of black people produced within,
and supported by, a racialized social order. However, what was
defined as authentic was a debate that was not easily resolved and
involved confrontation among black intellectuals themselves. Alain Locke, for example, who attempted to signal a change or a
break in conventions of representation by calling his collection of
the work of some Harlem intellectuals *The New Negro,* assumed
that the work of African-American intellectuals would be to raise
the culture of the folk to the level of art.[8] Locke's position has been
interpreted by contemporary critics as being very different from, if
not antagonistic to, the dominant interpretation of the work of
Hurston, who is thought to reconcile the division between "high
and low culture by becoming Eatonville's esthetic representative to
the Harlem Renaissance."[9]

In 1934, Hurston published an essay called "Spirituals and Neo-
spirituals" in which she argues that there had "never been a pre-
sentation of genuine Negro spirituals to any audience anywhere."

What was "being sung by the concert artists and glee clubs [were] the works of Negro composers or adaptors *based* on the spirituals."

> Glee clubs and concert singers put on their tuxedos, bow prettily to the audience, get the pitch and burst into magnificent song – but not *Negro* song. . . . let no one imagine that they are the songs of the people, as sung by them.[10]

Hurston was concerned to establish authenticity in the representation of popular forms of folk culture and to expose the disregard for the aesthetics of that culture through inappropriate forms of representation. She had no problem in using the term "the people" to register that she knew just who they were. But critics are incorrect to think that Hurston reconciled "high" and "low" forms of cultural production. Hurston's criticisms were not reserved for the elitist manner in which she thought the authentic culture of the people was reproduced. The people she wanted to represent she defined as a rural folk, and she measured them and their cultural forms against an urban, mass culture. She recognized that the people whose culture she rewrote were not the majority of the population, and that the cultural forms she was most interested in reproducing were not being maintained. She complained bitterly about how "the bulk of the population now spends its leisure in the motion picture theatres or with the phonograph and its blues." To Hurston, "race records" were nothing more than a commercialization of traditional forms of music, and she wanted nothing more to do with them.[11]

Understanding these *two* aspects of Hurston's theory of folk culture is important. When Hurston complained about the ways in which intellectuals transformed folk culture by reproducing and reinterpreting it as high culture, she identified a class contradiction. Most African-American intellectuals were generations removed from the "folk" they tried to represent. Their dilemma was little different from debates over proletarian fiction in the Soviet Union, in Europe, in the Caribbean, and in North America generally: debates that raged over the question of how and by whom should "the people," the masses of ordinary people, be portrayed.[12] Hurston identified herself as both an intellectual and as a representative figure from the folk culture she reproduced and made authentic in her work. However, asserting that she *was* both

75

did not resolve the contradictions embedded in the social meanings of each category. When Hurston complained about "race records" and the commercialization of the blues, she failed to apply her own analysis of processes of cultural transformation. On the one hand, she could argue that forms of folk culture were constantly reworked and remade when she stated that "the folk tales" like "the spirituals are being made and forgotten every day."[13] But, on the other hand, Hurston did not take seriously the possibility that African-American culture was being transformed as African-American peoples migrated from rural to urban areas.

The creation of a discourse of "the folk" as a *rural* people in Hurston's work in the 1920s and 1930s displaces the migration of black people to cities. Her representation of African-American culture as primarily rural and oral is Hurston's particular response to the dramatic transformations within black culture. It is these two processes that I am going to refer to as Hurston's discursive displacement of contemporary social crises in her writing. Hurston could not entirely escape the intellectual practice that she so despised, a practice that reinterpreted and redefined a folk consciousness in its own elitist terms. Hurston may not have dressed the spirituals in tuxedos but her attitude toward folk culture was not unmediated; she did have a clear framework of interpretation, a construct that enabled her particular representation of a black, rural consciousness.

Gayatri Spivak has pointed to an important dilemma in the issue of representing the subaltern. She sees "the radical intellectual in the West" as being caught either "in a deliberate choice of subalternity, granting to the oppressed . . . that very expressive subjectivity which s/he criticizes [in a post-structuralist theoretical world]" or, instead she faces the possibility of a total unrepresentability.[14] I don't know if the choice is always as bleak as Spivak claims, or is quite so simple and polarized. Langston Hughes, for example, in his use of the blues to structure poetry, represented a communal sensibility embedded in cultural forms and reproduced social meaning rather than individual subjectivity. In his blues poetry, the reader has access to a social consciousness through the reconstruction and representation of nonliterary, contemporary cultural forms that embodied the conditions of social transformation. Hurston, by contrast, assumed that she could obtain access to, and authenticate, an individualized social consciousness through a utopian reconstruction of the historical moment of her childhood in an attempt to stabilize and displace the social contradictions and disruption of her contemporary moment.

The issue of representing the subaltern, then, not only involves the relation of the intellectual to the represented, but also the relation of the intellectual to history. In Hurston's work, the rural black folk become an aesthetic principle, a means by which to embody a rich oral culture. Hurston's representation of the folk is not only a discursive displacement of the historical and cultural transformation of migration, but also is a creation of a folk who are outside of history. Hurston aggressively asserted that she was not of the "sobbing school of Negrohood" – in particular, to distinguish her work from that of Richard Wright – but she also places her version of authentic black cultural forms outside of the culture and history of contestation that informs his work. What the *New York Times* has recently called Hurston's "strong African-American sensibility" and is generally agreed to be her positive, holistic celebration of black life, also needs to be seen as a representation of "Negroness" as an unchanging, essential entity, an essence so distilled that it is an aesthetic position of blackness.

Hurston was a central figure in the cultural struggle among black intellectuals to define exactly who the people were that were going to become the representatives of the folk. Langston Hughes shaped his discursive category of the folk in direct response to the social conditions of transformation, including the newly forming urban working class and "socially dispossessed," whereas Hurston constructed a discourse of nostalgia for a rural community.[15] In her autobiographical writings, Hurston referenced the contradictory nature of the response of the black middle class and urban intellectuals to the presence of rural migrants to cities. In an extract written six months after completion of *Their Eyes Were Watching God*, Hurston describes this response:

> Say that a brown young woman, fresh from the classic halls of Barnard College and escorted by a black boy from Yale, enters the subway at 50th Street. They are well-dressed, well-mannered and good to look at. . . .

77

. . . the train pulls into 72nd Street. Two scabby-looking Negroes come scrambling into the coach. . . . but no matter how many vacant seats there are, no other place will do, except side by side with the Yale–Barnard couple. No, indeed! Being dirty and smelly, do they keep quiet otherwise? A thousand times, No! They woof, bookoo, broadcast. . . .

Barnard and Yale sit there and dwindle and dwindle. They do not look around the coach to see what is in the faces of the white passengers. They know too well what is there. . . . "That's just like a Negro." Not just like *some* Negroes, mind you, no, like all. Only difference is some Negroes are better dressed. Feeling all of this like rock-salt under the skin, Yale and Barnard shake their heads and moan, "My People, My People!" . . .

Certain of My People have come to dread railway day coaches for this same reason. They dread such scenes more than they do the dirty upholstery and other inconveniences of a Jim Crow coach. They detest the forced grouping. . . . So when sensitive souls are forced to travel that way they sit there numb and when some free soul takes off his shoes and socks, they mutter, "My race but not My taste." When somebody else eats fried fish, bananas, and a mess of peanuts and throws all the leavings on the floor, they gasp, "My skinfolks but not my kinfolks." And sadly over all, they keep sighing, "My People, My People!"[16]

This is a confrontation of class that signifies the division that the writer as intellectual has to recognize and bridge in the process of representing the people. It is a confrontation that was not unique to Hurston as intellectual, but it was one that she chose to displace in her decision to recreate Eatonville as the center of her representation of the rural folk.

The Eatonville of *Their Eyes Were Watching God* occupies a similar imaginative space to the mountain village of Banana Bottom in Claude McKay's novel of the same name published four years earlier.[17] McKay's Jamaican novel, set in the early 1900s, recreates the village where he grew up. Much of the argument of *Banana Bottom* emerges in the tension between attempts by missionaries to eradicate black cultural forms and the gentler forms of abuse present in white patronage of black culture. Against these forms of exploitation McKay reconstructs black culture as sustaining a whole way of life. But it is a way of life of the past, of his formative years, a place that the intellectual had to leave to become an intellectual and to which he does not return except in this Utopian moment. Eatonville, likewise, is the place of Hurston's childhood, a place to which she returns as an anthropologist. As she states in her introduction to *Mules and Men*, she consciously returns to the familiar,[18] and she recognizes that the stories she is going to collect, the ones she heard as a child, are a cultural form that is disappearing.[19]

In returning to and recreating the moment of her childhood, Hurston privileges the nostalgic and freezes it in time. Richard Wright, in his review of *Their Eyes Were Watching God*, accused Hurston of recreating minstrelsy. Though this remark is dismissed out of hand by contemporary critics, what it does register is Wright's reaction to what appears to him to be an outmoded form of historical consciousness. Whereas Wright attempted to explode the discursive category of the Negro as being formed, historically, in the culture of minstrelsy, and as being the product of a society structured in dominance through concepts of race, Hurston wanted to preserve the concept of Negroness, to negotiate and rewrite its cultural meanings, and, finally, to reclaim an aesthetically purified version of blackness. The consequences for the creation of subaltern subject positions in each of their works are dramatically different. The antagonism between them reveals Wright to be a modernist and leaves Hurston embedded in the politics of Negro identity.

Eatonville, as an anthropological and fictional space, appears in Hurston's work before her first anthropological expedition in 1927.[20] Not all the stories and anecdotes in *Mules and Men* originated from her research, and many appeared in different versions in different texts.[21] Rather than being valued primarily as a mode of scholarly inquiry, anthropology was important to Hurston because it enabled her to view the familiar and the known from a position of scientific objectivity, if not distance. She could not see her culture for wearing it, she said: "It was only when I was off in college, away from my native surroundings, that I could see myself like somebody else and stand off and look at my garment. Then I had to have the spy-glass of Anthropology to look through at that."[22] Anthropology, then, is seen by Hurston as providing a professional point of view. Ethnography becomes a tool in the creation of her discourse of the rural folk that displaces the antagonistic relations of cultural transformation.[23]

George Marcus and Michael Fischer have described the ways in which anthropology "developed the ethnographic paradigm" in the 1920s and 1930s. "Ethnographies as a genre," they argue, "had similarities with traveler and explorer accounts, in which the main narrative motif was the romantic discovery by the writer of people and places unknown to the reader."[24] Hurston shares this romantic and, it must be said, colonial imagination. Her representation of Eatonville in *Mules and Men* and in *Their Eyes Were Watching God* is both an attempt to make the unknown known and a nostalgic attempt to preserve a disappearing form of folk culture.[25] Marcus and Fischer argue that there are three dimensions to the criticism that ethnography offered of Western civilization:

[T]hey – primitive man – have retained a respect for nature, and we have lost it (the ecological Eden); they have sustained close, intimate, satisfying communal lives, and we have lost this way of life (the experience of community); and they have retained a sense of the sacred in everyday life, and we have lost this (spiritual vision).[26]

Whereas the other students of Franz Boas, Margaret Mead and Ruth Benedict, turned to societies outside of Europe and North America to point to what the West had lost but the cultural "other" still retained, Hurston's anthropological work concentrated upon the cultural "other" that existed within the racist order of North America.

In 1935, Ruth Benedict published *Patterns of Culture*, in which she asserted that black Americans were an example of what happens "when entire peoples in a couple of generations shake off their traditional culture and put on the customs of the alien group. The culture of the American Negro in northern cities," she continued, "has come to approximate in detail that of the whites in the same cities."[27] With this emphasis in the school of anthropological thought that most influenced Hurston, anthropology provided her with not only a "spyglass" but with a theoretical paradigm that directed her toward rural, not urban, black culture and folk forms of the past, not the present.

Hurston, like Benedict, was concerned with the relationships among the lives and cultures that she reconstructed and her own search for a construction of the self.[28] She lived the contradictions of the various constructions of her social identity and rewrote them in *Their Eyes Were Watching God*. Her anthropological "spyglass," which she trained on the society that produced her, allowed her to return to that society in the guise of being a listener and a reporter. In her fictional return, Hurston represents the tensions inherent in her position as an intellectual – in particular as a writer – in antagonistic relation to her construction of the folk as community. It is in this sense that I think Hurston is as concerned with the production of a sense of self as she is with the representation of a folk consciousness through its cultural forms. Both, I would argue, are the motivating forces behind the use of anthropological paradigms in Hurston's work. But it is the relation and tension between the two, particularly the intellectual consciousness and the consciousness of the folk, that is present in the fictional world of *Their Eyes Were Watching God*, which is written between her two books of anthropology, *Mules and Men* and *Tell My Horse*. In this novel, we can see how Hurston brings into being a folk consciousness that is actually in a contradictory relation to her sense of herself as an intellectual.

Throughout the 1930s, Hurston is in search of a variety of formal possibilities for the representation of black rural folk culture. She produced three musicals – *From Sun to Sun, The Great Day*, and *Singing Steel* – because she was convinced that folk culture should be dramatized. She returned to fiction as a form after a gap of six years when she wrote "The Gilded Six Bits" in 1933, and *Jonah's Gourd Vine*, which was published in 1934. Then Hurston seriously considered pursuing a Ph.D. degree at Columbia in anthropology and folklore. After finalizing all the arrangements for the publication of *Mules and Men*, however, Hurston accompanied Alan Lomax on a trip to collect folk music for the Library of Congress in 1935. That fall she joined the Federal Theatre Project and was prominent in organizing its Harlem unit as well as producing a one-act play, "The Fiery Chariot." Between 1936 and 1938, Hurston spent a major part of her time in the Caribbean collecting material on voodoo practices. She spent six months in Jamaica, and *Their Eyes Were Watching God* was written while she was in Haiti.[29] In *Their Eyes* she reproduces Eatonville from a distance which is both geographical and metaphorical and politically inscribed with issues of gender and class. Hurston's work during this

81

period, then, involves an intellectual's search for the appropriate forms in which to represent the folk and a decision to rewrite the geographical boundaries of representation by situating the southern, rural folk and patterns of migration in relation to the Caribbean rather than the northern states.

Henry Louis Gates, Jr. has explored the great detail matters of voice in *Their Eyes Were Watching God* in relation to a politics of identity by tracing Hurston's construction of a protagonist engaged in a search "to become a speaking black subject."[30] On the other hand, Mary Helen Washington and Robert Stepto have both raised intriguing questions about Janie's *lack* of voice in the text. Washington relates this silencing of a female protagonist to her reading of *Jonah's Gourd Vine* and concludes that "Hurston was indeed ambivalent about giving a powerful voice to a woman like Janie who is already in rebellion against male authority and against the roles prescribed for women in a male dominated society."[31] However, both sides of this debate about the speaking or silent subject exist within the same paradigm of voice. I wish to introduce an alternative paradigm that suggests ways in which *Their Eyes Were Watching God* is a text concerned with the tensions arising from Hurston's position as writer in relation to the folk as community that she produces in her writing. In other words, I want to concentrate upon the contradictions that arise in the relation between writer, as woman and intellectual, and her construction of subaltern subject positions rather than remain within critical paradigms that celebrate black identity.

The two chapters that frame the story of Janie's life and are central to arguments about the ways in which Hurston prepares the fictional space in which Janie can tell her own story actually detail the antagonistic relation between Janie, as a woman alone, and the folk as community. The community sits "in judgment" as the figure of Janie, the protagonist, walks through the town to her house. This walk can be seen as analogous to crossing a stage and "running the gauntlet." Oral language, as it was embodied in the folktale in *Mules and Men*, was a sign of an authentic culture that enabled a people to survive and even triumph spiritually over their oppression. In the opening chapter of *Their Eyes Were Watching God*, however, oral language is represented as a "weapon," a means for the destruction and fragmentation of the self rather than a cultural form that preserves a holistic personal and social identity. Questions become "burning statements," and laughs are "killing tools" (2). Janie has broken the boundaries of social convention and becomes the accused. She doesn't act appropriately for her age, which is "way past forty" (3). (Hurston was forty-five years old at the time the text was written, but on various occasions took between seven and nineteen years off her age.)[32] Also inappropriate are the class codes that Janie threatens in her behavior and in her dress: As a middle-class widow she should not have associated with the itinerant Tea Cake; and as a middle-class woman, her "faded shirt and muddy overalls" are a comforting sign to the folk as community who can ease their antagonism and resentment with the thought that maybe she will "fall to their level someday" (11).

Hurston increases the tension between her protagonist and the community to which she returns through a series of binary oppositions between the intellect, or mind, and speech. The process of the analysis by the anthropological self in *Mules and Men* is reversed by the creator of fiction in *Their Eyes Were Watching God*. In the former, the oral tale is a sign of a whole healthy culture and community; in the latter, the individual functions of speaking are isolated and lack a center. Janie responds to her victimization through synecdoche. The community is indicted as a "Mouth Almighty," a powerful voice that lacks intellectual direction. Far from being spiritually whole, the folk who are gathered on the porch are reduced to their various body parts: In each, an "envious heart makes a treacherous ear" (5).[33] This is the context that determines Janie's refusal to tell her story directly to the community, a refusal that distinguishes her story from the directly told and shared folktale. In the process of transmitting Janie's story, Hurston requires an instrument of mediation between her protagonist and the folk, and it is Janie's friend Pheoby who becomes this mediator. When Janie decides to tell her story through her friend – "Mah tongue is in mah friend's mouf" (5), she says – Hurston creates a figure for the form of the novel, a fictional world that can mediate and perhaps resolve the tension that exists in the difference between the socially constructed identities of "woman" and "intellectual" and the act of representing the folk.[34]

Hurston's particular form of mediation appears to be an alternative version of the anthropological spyglass that she needed to create a professional point of view between her consciousness of self and the subjects she was reproducing. Janie's definite refusal to tell her tale directly, as in a folktale, distinguishes not only her story from other stories that are communally shared, but also her position from that of the folk as community. Hurston's position as intellectual is reproduced as a relation of difference, as an antagonistic relationship between Janie and the folk. The lack in the folk figures, the absence of mind, or intellectual direction in the porch sitters, is symbolically present when Janie mounts her own porch.

In *Mules and Men,* the porch is the site for the expression of the folktale as an evocation of an authentic black culture. In *Their Eyes Were Watching God,* the porch is split and transformed. Whereas in *Mules and Men* the anthropological self is positioned on a figuratively unified porch, primarily as a listener and a recorder, in *Their Eyes Were Watching God* the anthropological role of listener is embedded in the folk as community and the role of recorder situated in the mediator – Pheoby/the text. In the novel, then, a listening *audience* is established for the narrative self, whereas in *Mules and Men* Hurston constructs a listening *anthropological subject.* It is Janie who can address and augment the lack in the folk as community and Janie who can unify the division between mind and mouth. Janie, of course, is placed in the subject position of intellectual and has the desire to "sit down and tell [the folk] things." Janie, as intellectual, has traveled outside of the community and defines herself as "a delegate to de big 'ssociation of life" (6); her journey is the means by which knowledge can be brought into the community. As intellectual she creates subjects, grants individual consciousness, and produces understanding – the cultural meanings without which the tale is useless to the community – "taint no use in me telling you somethin' unless Ah give you de understandin' to go 'long wid it," Janie tells Pheoby. The conscious way in which subjectivity is shaped and directed is the act of mediation of the writer; it is this sense in which Pheoby becomes both Hurston's instrument of mediation and her text in an act of fictionalization.

The second part of the frame in the last chapter of *Their Eyes Were*

Watching God opens with the resolution of the tension, division, and antagonism that are the subject of the opening chapter. The pattern of division of the first part of the frame is repeated: Janie is verbally condemned by the folk as community because she killed Tea Cake. The folk "lack" the understanding of the reasoning behind Janie's actions, but this deficiency is compensated for only through Janie's defense of herself in a court of law. The folk on the muck finally end their hostility to Janie when Sop explains that Tea Cake went crazy and Janie acted to protect herself. Reconciliation, then, between the position of intellectual and the folk as community takes place through acts of narration. The discursive unity that is maintained in the framing of the text prefigures the possibility for reconciliation between the position of Janie, as both intellectual and woman, and the folk as community when Pheoby provides them with the understanding of Janie's life through what will be another act of narration. *Their Eyes Were Watching God*, as such an act of narration itself, offers a resolution to the tension between Hurston, as intellectual, as writer, and the people she represents. In a paragraph that reproduces the tension in relation of the intellectual to the folk Hurston specifies the source of antagonism between Janie and the community as being a lack of knowledge.

> Now, Pheoby, don't feel too mean wid de rest of 'em 'cause dey's parched up from not knowin' things. Dem meatskins is *got* tuh rattle tuh make out they's alive. Let 'em consolate theyselves wid talk. 'Course, talkin' don't amount tuh uh hill uh beans when yuh can't do nothin' else. And listenin' tuh dat kind uh talk is jus' lak openin' yo' mouth and lettin' de moon shine down yo' throat. It's uh known fact, Pheoby, you got tuh *go* there tuh *know* there. Yo' papa and yo' mama and nobody else can't tell yuh and show yuh. Two things everybody's got tuh do fuh theyselves. They got tuh go tuh God, and they got tuh find out about livin' fuh theyselves. (183)

The passage that I have quoted here is the final paragraph in Janie's story. It gains authority from claiming the tone of the preacher and the pedagogue, and at the same time it evokes the dilemma of the intellectual. Hurston's journey away from the community that produced her and that she wants to reproduce has provided her with a vision of an alternative world. Although it is not actually present in the text, the novel ends with the possibility

that that history could be brought into the community and suggests that Pheoby/the text is the means for accomplishing the
transformation necessary to reconcile difference. However, as a
woman and as an intellectual, Hurston has to negotiate both gendered and classed constructions of social identity and subjec-
tivities.

Critics often forget that Janie is a protagonist whose subject
position is defined through class, that she can speak on a porch
because she *owns* it. The contradictions between her appearance in
overalls, a sign of material lack, and the possession of nine hundred dollars in the bank are important. Hurston's anthropological
trips for *Mules and Men* were financed by a patron, Mrs. Osgood
Mason, to whom she dedicates the text. The folklore material that
Hurston had collected she could not freely utilize as she wished:
Mason had made it abundantly clear that she claimed proprietary
ownership of all that ethnographic material. Hurston traveled to
Jamaica and Haiti on her own Guggenheim grant, and, when she
was writing *Their Eyes*, she must have pleasured in the sense that
no one else could claim ownership of her words and her work.
However, the problem is that providing her protagonist with the
financial independence that Hurston herself must have found necessary in order to occupy a position from which to write reinforces
the division between Janie and her community. The text here
echoes Janie's grandmother's demand for a place like the white
woman's, a place on high. The fact that Janie does indeed mount
and own her porch enables the story, but also permeates it with a
bourgeois discourse that differentiates her from the folk as community.

But this intellectual and property owner is also a woman, and
thus the problem of representation here is also a question of how a
woman can write her story within a site that is male-dominated
and patriarchally defined. In *Mules and Men*, Hurston addresses the
social constitution of gender roles in particular tales and through
brief narratives that describe the relations among the tale-tellers on
the porch, but she does not inscribe a concern with gender within
the terms of the professional role of the anthropologist itself.[35]
However, the role of listener had its limitations. Hurston's conscious reversal of the role of anthropologist reveals the contradic-

tions inherent in the processes through which an intellectual, an intellectual who is also a woman, can instruct a community about what is outside of its social consciousness. This is the problem that frames the novel. The final metaphor of the horizon as a "great fish-net" with "so much of life in its meshes" (184) that Janie pulls in and drapes around herself is an appropriate image for a writer who can recreate and represent a social order in her narrative. But what this metaphor also confirms is the distance between the act of representation and the subjects produced through that act of representation. The assertion of autonomy implicit in this figuration of a discourse that exists only for the pleasure of the self displaces the folk as community utterly and irrevocably.

I have suggested ways in which the narrative strategies of *Mules and Men* and *Their Eyes Were Watching God* are different and yet similar in that they both evoke the romantic imagination so characteristic of ethnography in the 1930s. If, as Marcus and Fischer suggest, the main narrative motif of ethnography is the "romantic discovery by the writer of people and places unknown to the reader," then *Mules and Men* both discovers the rural folk and acts to make known and preserve a form of culture that embodies a folk consciousness. The folk as community remain the "other" and exist principally as an aesthetic device, a means for creating an essential concept of blackness. The framing of that novel is the process of working out, or mapping, a way of writing and discovering the subject position of the intellectual in relation to what she represents.

Hurston's journey to Jamaica and two trips to Haiti produced *Tell My Horse*, a text that Robert Hemenway has dismissed as Hurston's "poorest book." Hemenway argues that Hurston "was a novelist and folklorist, not a political analyst or traveloguist."[36] I would agree that Hurston's overtly political comments in *Tell My Horse* are usually reactionary, blindly patriotic, and, consequently, superficial. The dominant tendency in Hurston scholarship has been to ignore or dismiss as exceptional some of her more distasteful political opinions but, as Marcus and Fischer have explained, the ethnology and travelogue share a romantic vision (and I would add a colonial or imperial vision), making *Tell My Horse* not an exception to Hurston's work at this moment in her life but an integral part of it. In the second chapter of Part Two of *Mules and Men*, the section entitled "Hoodoo," Hurston shifts away from a concern to record and preserve a particular form of black culture, the folktale, and toward a desire to create the boundaries of a cultural world in a relation of difference to the dominant culture. The geographical boundaries of Hurston's black folk are rural, but their Southern-ness is not defined through a difference to Northernness as much as it is related to cultural practices and beliefs of the Caribbean. This shift is clear when Hurston, the anthropologist, moves from Florida to New Orleans and seeks to become a pupil of a "hoodoo doctor."[37]

In her introduction to *Mules and Men*, Hurston explains that she chose Florida as a site for the collection of folklore not only because it was familiar, but because she saw Florida as "a place that draws people . . . Negroes from every Southern state . . . and some from the North and West. So I knew it was possible for me to get a cross section of the Negro South in one state."[38] In the section of *Mules and Men* that is situated in Louisiana, we can see a shift in Hurston's work to a stress on a continuity of cultural beliefs and practices with beliefs and practices in the Caribbean. In *Their Eyes Were Watching God* this system of reference is continued through the way in which Hurston discursively displaces the urban migration of black people in the continental United States. In her novel, as in *Mules and Men*, migration is from the Southern states further south to Eatonville, Florida. Migration in a northerly direction is undertaken only by the Barbadians who join Janie and Tea Cake on the "muck." After the completion of her novel, Hurston continued her search for an appropriate vehicle for the expression of black culture in *Tell My Horse* – a first-person account of her travels in Jamaica and Haiti. Part Three of *Tell My Horse* completes the journey, initiated in *Mules and Men*, in search of the survival of the ritual and practices of Vodoun.[39]

The geographic boundaries that enclose *Their Eyes Were Watching God* enlarge our understanding of the metaphoric boundaries of self and community. The discourse of the folk, which I have argued is irrevocably displaced in the figuration of a discourse of individualized autonomy existing only for the pleasure of the self, is dispersed and fragmented in a narrative of Hurston's personal initiation into African religious practices in the diaspora. Hurston does not return again to a romantic vision of the folk. Her next book, *Moses, Man of the Mountain*, is an extension of her interest in the relations between and across black cultures because it rewrites in fictional terms the worship of Moses and the worship of Damballah that had first interested her in Haiti.[40] This figuration of Moses/Damballah also transforms questions about the relation of the intellectual to the folk as community into an exploration of the nature of leaders and leadership. The intricate inquiry into the construction of subject positions, as writer, as woman, and as intellectual, is also not repeated. In *Dust Tracks on a Road*, an apparently autobiographical act, Hurston ignores her earlier attempts to represent the complexity of the relationship between public and private constructions of the self. She continues, however, to displace the discourse of a racist social order and maintains the exclusion of the black subject from history. This is the gesture that eventually wins her the recognition and admiration of the dominant culture in the form of the Anisfield–Wolf Award for the contribution of *Dust Tracks on a Road* to the field of race relations.[41]

We need to return to the question why, at this particular moment in our society, *Their Eyes Were Watching God* has become such a privileged text. Why is there a shared assumption that we should read the novel as a positive, holistic, celebration of black life? Why is it considered necessary that the novel produce cultural meanings of authenticity, and how does cultural authenticity come to be situated so exclusively in the rural folk?

I would like to suggest that, as cultural critics, we could begin to acknowledge the complexity of our own discursive displacement of contemporary conflict and cultural transformation in the search for black cultural authenticity. The privileging of Hurston at a moment of intense urban crisis and conflict is, perhaps, a sign of that displacement: Large parts of black urban America under siege; the number of black males in jail in the 1980s doubled; the news media have recently confirmed what has been obvious to many of us for some time – that one in four young black males are in prison, on probation, on parole, or awaiting trial; and young black children face the prospect of little, inadequate, or no health care. Has *Their Eyes Were Watching God* become the most frequently taught black novel because it acts as a mode of assurance that, really, the black folk are happy and healthy?

Richard Wright has recently been excluded from contemporary formations of the African-American canon because he brought into fictional consciousness the subjectivity of a *Native Son* created in conditions of aggression and antagonism,[42] but, perhaps, it is time that we should question the extent of our dependence upon the romantic imagination of Zora Neale Hurston to produce cultural meanings of ourselves as native daughters.

NOTES

1. I would like to thank Richard Yarborough for his helpful suggestions and corrections made to an earlier version of this manuscript. The editions cited in the text are as follows: Robert E. Hemenway, *Zora Neale Hurston: A Literary Biography* (Urbana: University of Illinois Press, 1977); Zora Neale Hurston, *Their Eyes Were Watching God* (New York: Harper and Row, 1990); Hurston, *Dust Tracks on a Road* (New York: Harper and Row, 1990); Hurston, *Mules and Men: Negro Folktales and Voodoo Practices in the South* (New York: Harper and Row, 1990); Hurston, *Tell My Horse* (New York: Harper and Row, 1990).
2. Personal communication with Henry Louis Gates, Jr. (February 1990).
3. Rosemary L. Bray, "Renaissance for a Pioneer of Black Pride," *New York Times* (February 4, 1990).
4. A more detailed consideration of this parallel would need to examine what Nelson George calls "selling race." The ability of the record industry to market and make a profit from "black talent performing black music" in the 1920s could be interestingly compared to the highly profitable publishing of the work of black women writers, the Book of the Month Club's distribution of Alice Walker's novel, *The Color Purple*, and the subsequent film of the same name, and the success of Spike Lee's *She's Gotta Have It* and *School Daze*. See Nelson George, *The Death of Rhythm and Blues* (New York: Pantheon, 1988), pp. 8–9.
5. Hazel V. Carby, *Reconstructing Womanhood: The Emergence of the Afro-American Woman Novelist* (New York: Oxford University Press, 1987), pp. 163–6.
6. Edward W. Said, "Representing the Colonized: Anthropology's Interlocutors," *Critical Inquiry* 15 (Winter 1989): 205–6.

Fiction, Anthropology, and the Folk

7. See Gayatri Chakravorty Spivak, *In Other Worlds: Essays in Cultural Politics* (New York: Methuen, 1987), pp. 197–221. Spivak identifies and elaborates upon the concern of the work of subaltern studies with change as "confrontations rather than transition" and the marking of change through "function changes in sign systems." This rather awkward phrase, "function changes in sign systems," becomes in the process of Spivak's analysis the somewhat shorter phrase "discursive displacements."
8. See, for example, Hemenway, *Zora Neale Hurston*, p. 50.
9. Ibid., p. 56.
10. Hurston, "Spirituals and Neo-spirituals," in *The Sanctified Church* (Berkeley, CA: Turtle Island, 1981), pp. 80–1.
11. Hemenway, *Zora Neale Hurston*, p. 92.
12. See Hazel V. Carby, "Proletarian or Revolutionary Literature: C. L. R. James and the Politics of the Trinidadian Renaissance," *South Atlantic Quarterly* 87 (Winter 1988): 39–52.
13. Hurston, "Spirituals and Neo-spirituals," p. 79.
14. Spivak, *In Other Worlds*, p. 209.
15. See Ralph Ellison, "Recent Negro Fiction," *New Masses* 40 (August 5 1941): 22–6.
16. Hurston, *Dust Tracks on a Road*, pp. 292–4.
17. Claude McKay, *Banana Bottom* (New York: Harper & Row, 1933).
18. Hurston, *Mules and Men*, pp. 17–19.
19. Ibid., p. 24.
20. See Hurston, "The Eatonville Anthology," *Messenger* 8 (Sept., Oct., Nov., 1926): 261–2, 297, 319, 332.
21. See Arnold Rampersad's comments in his introduction to the new edition of *Mules and Men* (New York: Harper and Row, 1990), pp. xxii–xxiii.
22. Hurston, *Mules and Men*, p. 17.
23. See Hemenway, *Zora Neale Hurston*, p. 221, who calls this reconstruction of Eatonville idealized but feels that Hurston chose to assert positive images "because she did not believe that white injustice had created a pathology in black behavior." I remain unconvinced by this argument because it simplifies to a level of binary oppositions between positive and negative images what are very complex processes of representation. It is interesting that Hemenway seems to realize this inadequacy in the next paragraph when he raises but cannot resolve the problem of "professional colonialism" in Hurston's anthropological stance.
24. George E. Marcus and Michael E. Fischer, *Anthropology as Cultural*

91

Critique: An Experimental Moment in the Human Sciences (Chicago: University of Chicago Press, 1986), pp. 129, 24.

25. Hurston's desire to make black people and culture known is evident in letters she wrote to James Weldon Johnson. See Zora Neale Hurston to James Weldon Johnson, January 22, 1934, in which she complains that the J. B. Lippincott Company is "not familiar with Negroes"; and May 8, 1934, in which she says about the review of Jonah's Gourd Vine in the New York Times that she "never saw such a lack of information about us." Both letters are in the James Weldon Johnson Collection, Beinecke Library, Yale University.

26. Marcus and Fischer, Anthropology as Cultural Critique, p. 129.

27. Ruth Benedict, Patterns of Culture (Boston: Houghton Mifflin, 1934), p. 13.

28. See Margaret Mead's introduction to Patterns of Culture, written in 1958, which opens the 1959 edition, p. ix.

29. Hemenway, Zora Neale Hurston, pp. 184–5, 202–27, 230.

30. Henry Louis Gates, Jr., The Signifying Monkey: A Theory of Afro-American Literary Criticism (New York: Oxford University Press, 1988), pp. 170–216.

31. Mary Helen Washington, Invented Lives: Narratives of Black Women 1860–1960 (New York: Doubleday, 1987), p. 245. Washington's re-reading of Their Eyes Were Watching God is an admirable analysis of the ways in which this text has been romanticized, and initiates the important work of comparative analysis across texts. It was this essay that first encouraged and inspired me to follow her lead and think seriously of the relations between Hurston's texts. See also Robert Stepto, From Behind the Veil: A Study of Afro-American Narrative (Urbana: University of Illinois Press, 1979), pp. 164–7.

32. See Hemenway's introduction to the second edition of Dust Tracks on a Road, p. xi.

33. I am grateful to Richard Yarborough for pointing out to me that of course, this aphorism is itself drawn from oral tradition. My emphasis is that in its application at this point in the novel, it stresses division.

34. I am implicitly arguing, therefore, that it is necessary to step outside questions of voice and issues of third-person (as opposed to first-person) narration in order to understand why Hurston needs an instrument of mediation between the teller of the tale and the tale itself.

35. This may have been because other women like Mead and Benedict were also using the role of anthropologist as a position from which to accumulate knowledge that was both authoritative and scientific. But this is just a guess. The relations among these three anthropologists

have not been explored, as far as I know, but a comparative examination of the nature of their work would seem to be an interesting area for future study.

36. Hemenway, *Zora Neale Hurston*, pp. 248–9.
37. Hurston, *Mules and Men*, p. 239.
38. Ibid., p. 17.
39. It would be fruitful to explore the relationship between Hurston's interest in and use of the Caribbean in these years with the cultural production of intellectuals who turned to the Caribbean, in particular the island of Haiti, as a source for an alternative revolutionary black history. I am thinking here, among other works, of the production of the play *Touissant L'Ouverture* by C. L. R. James, which opened in London in March 1936 starring Paul Robeson, and the publication, in 1938, of *Black Jacobins;* Jacob Lawrence's series of paintings on Touissant L'Ouverture, 1937–8; Langston Hughes's *Troubled Island* written for, but never produced by, the Federal Theatre; and the New York Negro Federal Theatre production of *Macbeth*, often referred to as the "voodoo" *Macbeth*, directed by Orson Welles in 1936. Other black units in the Federal Theatre performed *Black Empire* by Christine Ames and Clarke Painter, and *Haiti* by William Du Bois, a journalist for the *New York Times*.
40. Hurston, *Tell My Horse*, pp. 139–40.
41. Hemenway, "Introduction" to Hurston, *Dust Tracks*, p. ix.
42. See Henry Louis Gates, Jr., *The Signifying Monkey: A Theory of Afro-American Literary Criticism*, pp. 118–20 and 181–4.

5

Power, Judgment, and Narrative in a Work of Zora Neale Hurston: Feminist Cultural Studies

RACHEL BLAU DuPLESSIS

1

THE first time we see the hero/ine of *Their Eyes Were Watching God*, she is sauntering down a road, the knowing subject of gossiping judgment. Janie is an expressively sexual woman (her buttocks and "pugnacious breasts" are immediately mentioned). She is black, but her "great rope of black hair" operates as a marker of her racial mix, and an evocation of the internal color lines in the African-American community.[1] She is all of forty – too old, according to her neighbors, collectively termed "Mouth-Almighty," to change, adventure, or express sexuality. And finally, her overalls are a nice bit of cross-dressing, signifying equality and sexuality in gender terms, and in class terms signifying her double class status as property (petty-bourgeois – local notable) annealed to "poverty" (agricultural day worker). Janie can be seen from the very first moments of the novel to be made of signs, like "Alphabet," her childhood nickname. These signs of Janie are constructed by Hurston to be conflictual and heterogeneous in the array of race, gender role, age, class, and sexual markers.[2] However, as the early incident of the photograph pointedly tells, the multiplicity and plurality of "Alphabet" are focused suddenly: "Aw, aw! Ah'm colored!" (9). The paradox of Janie – her fascination – is Hurston's narrating Janie's efforts to spell her life with more than that one word "colored," while necessarily, her life is focused by the social, economic, and cultural meanings of blackness. Race is first, or primary, yet at the same time race exists among many social deter-

95

minants. Analyzing the narrative and textual interplay and effects of these multiple determinants is the task of feminist cultural studies.

Janie is in an incessant dialogue with the meanings of "colored," of which she is not in control. To construct Janie's dialogue, Hurston has treated many of these social determinants (such as class, sexuality, and gender role) as if they were matters of choice and risk for her character, not fixed and immobilized. Hurston's presumption of Janie's choice in coping with social determinants is an assumption she also makes in her autobiography, *Dust Tracks on a Road*. There her basic attitude is that my race is part of the hand I have been dealt; now I will play it. Race is something with which to be strategic. Her race is not "a low-down dirty deal"; she is not, as she tersely informs us, either a self-pitying or a "tragically colored" person.[3] Her scathing critique of the unifying fervors of Race Pride, Race Consciousness, and Race Solidarity, and her scathing contempt for anti-Negro racial prejudice match each other. She wants an end to binary thinking about race. She is in favor of "seeking individual capabilities and depths," a proposal that occurs upon her nonetheless inescapable material ground of racially situated rural poverty, early bereavement, family scattering and anger, and scrabbling for education and employment.[4]

Hurston wants to analyze race without being reduced to race. In the title "How It Feels To Be Colored Me," she makes a distinction between "it" and "me"; by saying that she is not "it," she implies that her ego, her "me" is informed by, yet not reduced to her race. Yet "colored me" is in the object case, not the subject form, suggesting the impact of objectification on her in spite of herself. To echo an image Hurston uses in the novel, there is an "inside" and an "outside" to Hurston's rhetorical choice, and although she uses this image of unmasking (an "I will tell you how it feels"), still the word "it" does mask things. By saying "I have no separate feelings about being an American citizen and colored," she provides a critical reply to DuBois's influential analysis of African-Americans' double consciousness. Yet sometimes she insists that she feels "*so* colored," thus constitutively African-American; at other times she implies she is just one among many differently hued human "bags" with their diversified contents, separating one's outside color and one's real insides.[5]

Because Janie is constructed of dialogic play among multiple social factors, Hurston's hero/ine provokes a critic toward this feminist imperative: the critical analysis of multiple social determinants in their narrative meanings. Gynocriticism – the study of women writers – has been in a divided state virtually since it was first defined. If it is gynocentrist and polarizing in its assumptions (as in reasserting cultural stereotypes, fixed definitions of gender behavior, wars between the sexes, or static, transhistorical gender categories), it will be writing a story of dominance versus otherness which seems finally to have a religious plot of a victim transformed by celebratory glorification. But there has always been a gynocriticism emphasizing the cultural analysis of texts. Still, in Elaine Showalter's summarizing statement in "Feminist Criticism in the Wilderness," one is engaged with a special kind of fruitful tension. Showalter calls for feminist criticism as cultural studies; understanding "differences between women as writers: class, race, nationality, and history are literary determinants as significant as gender."[6] Yet Showalter goes on immediately to propose that in this ensemble of practices, gender is primary, and "women's culture" still has a "binding force." Several similar formulations follow, each using slightly different metaphors. Showalter sees gender as the most constitutive among multiple strata, and sees other factors as intersections on a field primarily formed by gender. How can one both hold to gender – as a feminist critic – and release it to function in a network or ensemble of factors that is not controlled by a more privileged "binding" element? For feminist criticism is historically well placed to contribute to a criticism of social determinants in their relation to representation and ideology – in short, cultural studies.[7] But to do so one has to situate the feminism most comfortably in the critic, and be agnostic about whether a specific text or author makes gender primary. Feminist cultural studies are those discussions of social ensembles made in specific by a *feminist* critic who encourages, as Nancy Miller does, one particular task of overreading.[8] To have isolated gender solely and totally was a practice necessary for the origins of feminist criticism. But now, the impact and meanings of gender must be explored contextually. Feminist cultural studies will produce analyses of the multiple social forces at issue in cultural activity, especially as those are seen textually, in narrative and image.

Three necessary engagements enable this kind of criticism. First, following Lillian Robinson, we must reaffirm and repractice a break with kinds of social privilege expressed in (or as) "literary criticism," especially the privilege of disinterested scrutiny of something other, in which we claim we are not implicated. For example, taking the social determinants of race, gender, class, and sexualities, a critic must deeply acknowledge that race is not exclusive to blacks (or other "minorities"); gender is not exclusive to women; class is not exclusive to working people; sexualities are not limited to gays, lesbians, and bisexuals.[9] That is, to look only at the marked group's markers is to replay certain ideological polarizations by which powerholders (women among them) never question themselves as markable, or see themselves as speaking socially inflected, ideological texts.

A white critic looking at Hurston could see her Negroness as marked, and will want to elaborate her attitudes toward that race in isolation from all other factors, including the critic's own assumptions about blackness and whiteness. But Hurston has a decided racial bifocality. The narrative memories and patterns of *Dust Tracks* show Hurston being (and narrating herself as) a participant in both black and white worlds, show the degree to which she was equally touched by black and white people, the degree to which both black and white were powerful generative forces in her life. The (mainly) positive connections to whites which Hurston chooses to narrate (as I, a white person, see this) began at Hurston's birth, for she was "grannied" by a white man (*DT* 29–30), who remained friendly through her childhood. He instructed her, "Don't be a nigger." She thus learned that the word "nigger" could sometimes mean class and values, not race (*DT* 41).[10] Her paean to friendship is a perfectly even-handed tribute in which she treats both white and black: Fannie Hurst and Ethel Waters. It is a chapter significantly titled "Two Women in Particular" and set after the "My People! My People!" agglomeration, as if to prove that it was always the specificity of individuals that mattered and not their race (*DT* 238–248). About slavery she pointedly notes

98

bifurcated responsibility: "My people had *sold* me and the white people had bought me" (*DT* 200). And the final paragraph of her autobiography is a beneficent extension of herself as a model world-citizen, pleasantly inviting high and low, black and white: "Let us all be kissing-friends" (*DT* 286). Hurston might have been narrating a higher degree of racial cooperation than one might expect in America, narrating her version of social progress, narrating an interpretation of her genius transcending race.

In a feminist program of cultural studies, each social determinant must be seen multifocally, conflictually, and over time. In a challenge toward feminist criticism to work with multiple systems of social difference to examine how race, class, and gender constitute themselves in interaction and dialogue, the critic Cora Kaplan insists that none of the "social determinants" is itself unitary and unconflictual, and that all are the results of ongoing discursive practices as well as ongoing social relations.[11] Hurston offers clear evidence, for she had a very complex and conflictual picture of her race. Hurston sees "Negroness" first as a material fact of course involving marked social prejudice which it was in her interest and in her capacity to transcend. "It would be against all nature for all the Negroes to be either at the bottom, top, or in between. It has never happened with anybody else, so why with us? No, we will go where the internal drive carries us like everybody else. It is up to the individual. If you haven't got it, you can't show it. If you have got it, you can't hide it" (*DT* 237). Hurston offers this "genius theory" in defiance of the invisible shackles of institutionalized race and economic prejudice. Second, Hurston sees her race as a determinant that itself could be overruled by class and economic self-interest. She discusses the attempt of a black man to cross the Jim Crow color line in a black-owned and black-run barber shop in which Hurston was a manicurist, a shop designed to serve whites only. He gets thrown out by the black owner and workers. She says she "realized I was giving sanction to Jim Crow, which theoretically, I was supposed to resist." But she concludes that these actions exemplified economic self-interest (*DT* 162–5). Third, Hurston sees her race as a cultural heritage it was her destiny and conscious glory to embody. She repeatedly speaks of the folk sources of her art, and, in an often-cited, succinct credo, said about her specific relation with her patron, but really all her art: "I must tell the tales, sing the songs, do the dances, and repeat the raucous sayings and doings of the Negro farthest down" (*DT* 177). This aesthetic position is a conscious repudiation of the "better-thinking Negro" who "wanted nothing to do with anything frankly Negroid. . . . The Spirituals, the Blues, *any* definitely Negroid thing was just not done" (*DT* 233). Fourth, Hurston sees race as a falsely universalizing category: "There is no *The Negro* here" (*DT* 237). In the course of her remarkable chapter on the class divisions in the Negro community ("My People! My People!"), Hurston remarks, "Light came to me when I realized that I did not have to consider any racial group as a whole" (*DT* 235).[12] To try to say how Hurston regarded her race is hardly to propose a simple answer.

To try to say how the whites around her saw her race is also to propose a conflictual ensemble of white views of blackness. The white person who most decisively influenced her during the period before she wrote *Their Eyes Were Watching God* was the patron who also patronized her, and who may have passively discouraged her from writing the novel. Mrs. Mason took a specific kind of pleasure in all her black friends: She liked them to manifest what she "knew" as the deep and essential structure of their being: primitiveness. This concept seems to be a repeated concern in white vanguardist artistic and social communities (Lawrence comes to mind). To the degree that this a priori assumption is an awkward way of stating an interest in African survivals in the diaspora, it is a plausible hypothesis about black culture in the Americas. This still shows how important positional difference is to the articulation of ideas – for it is one thing for African-American writers to assume the "primitive and intuitive" as a badge of pride and common identity, and it is quite another – indeed, a form of colonization – for a white person to insist that blacks manifest these traits above all others. And to the degree that Mason's insistence that the primitive was the sole black authenticity "savagely" stereotypes heterogeneousness and compromises the individuality of African-Americans, we can only call her interest a kind of racism.[13]

Finally, feminist cultural studies would attempt to isolate crucial moments when a reader understands the interplay of social contexts and narrative texts. For example, it might be plausible to see Hurston's multiple occasions for making stories (orally in "personal performance," in short stories, in drama, in novels, in autobiography) as a construction of author as a tribal teller of tales. She did not especially alter the stories told, but she did alter the audiences to which and the narrative contexts in which the stories occurred. The multiple tellings are then replicas of the folklore situation, as if different "versions" of a tale could occur, none final, settled, or fixed despite being in a given work of art.[14] This writing tactic across her career challenges the boundaries of a work of art, and is thus a strategy of the African-American "deformation of mastery" by at once making a finished (bounded) work and re-dissolving its materials into a folk pool. Her tactic is also, arguably, a critique of hegemonic tactics of story-making by a version of the "delegitimation" characteristic of the gendered poetics of critique. Specifically African-American and feminist critical practices shed related cross-lights on her art.[15]

Feminist cultural studies would foreground the interplay of as many social determinants as can be justly, and imaginatively, seen first in the text – in narrative choices, structures, systems, outcomes, and tropes – and second, in the web of circumstances surrounding a text, especially its fabrication and its reception.[16] This kind of critical agenda leads finally to those textual moments when multiple social determinants seem to have concrete impact on narrative materials.

Their Eyes Were Watching God is structured in such a way as to reserve judgment to or for the black community, and most particularly to whomever might be construed as "the Negro farthest down" in any situation (*DT* 177). The most melodramatic and satisfying moment occurs in the notable confrontation of Joe by Janie in an exchange that ends with her decisive remark, "You look lak de change uh life" (75). In this novel, any kind of bullying is undercut by whoever is a "cut under": Sop-de-Bottom and Tea Cake undercut Mis Turner; Janie undercuts Joe; mules undercut men.

But this active pattern occurs not only in local scenes. It is the motor that runs the whole narrative structure with its framing of the quest and romance plots. The undercutting in particular accounts for significant moments when Janie's speech is depicted by Hurston but indirectly, or "silently" – as in the courtroom scene. Hurston achieves this appropriation of judgment to "the Negro furthest down" even though whites do have, and must be depicted as having, more political, legal, and extralegal powers of judgment, and even though black judgment (the wisdom of the community or its members) often runs strongly against Janie. The trial scene is the main place in which race and gender (as well as class and sexuality) – an ensemble of social forces – show intense cross-purposes and mutual conflicts in their narrative impact.

One must begin thinking through the trial scene by recalling that after the hurricane Tea Cake and Janie decide to return to the muck, on the principle, laughingly discussed, that the whites who know you are better than the whites who don't because of the structure of prejudice brought down to its basic component – prejudgment: "De ones de white man know is nice colored folks. De ones he don't know is bad niggers" (164). Tea Cake has just slid away from a press gang burying the dead. Soon after, his symptoms of rabies become unmistakable, Janie has a foreshadowing moment: "Ah loves him fit tuh kill" (168). The scene of the shooting is very carefully structured by Hurston, in every detail exculpatory: Tea Cake's mind gone paranoid, his pistol already loaded to try to kill her, and Janie shifting the bullets in the chambers in self-protection; her rifle put at readiness; the clear aggression of the rabid man, his three "false shots" (the three blank chambers), her warnings and attempts to stop him, and the final simultaneous and mutual shots, where Janie – as has been carefully noted before – is a better shot than he. He dies in the position of biting her.

This careful choreography of realistic, foregrounded dialogue and precisely delineated action is immediately followed by the trial scene, a blurry, dreamlike, bizarre scene, imprecise in inception ("she must be tried that same day" is to the highest degree unlikely), choral and diffuse by its end. White men are the jury and judges, the prosecuting attorney and the defense attorney. They are all strangers (the word "strange" recurs, too, and the tone of the indirect narrative is estranged). They "didn't know a thing about people like Tea Cake and her" (274) – Hurston's innocent-voiced irony about a "jury of one's peers." These strange, stranger whites have little interest in the issues, but they have the power to define fact and procedure: to "pass on what happened" and "as to whether things were done right or not."

The main interests of the white men are served by their intense blast at one of Tea Cake's angry friends. For his attempt to intervene in the "white man's procedures" and to use "the only real weapon left to weak folks," the "only killing tool they are allowed to use in the presence of white folks" – the power of speech (which is described in gunlike terms: "tongues cocked and loaded," 176) – Sop-de-Bottom is silenced and threatened with the law. The interest of white men in this trial is to contain and disempower the rage of the black male community. However, white men are also depicted as being brought to a realization of the deep meaning of the marriage of Tea Cake and Janie by the power of Janie's own testimony: that is, they are forced to acknowledge the sexual-relational feelings (the "humanity") of their social, and racial, "inferiors." The trial is a conversion experience for whites in their crediting part of the experience of blacks: they appreciate romance, but not forms of political outrage. My response (as a white critic) is that whites have gotten off easier than is plausible by virtue of the commanding stature with which Hurston has invested her hero/ine, but also (possibly) because of Hurston's own charitable asocial attitude toward the constitutive nature of prejudice which allows her to depict Janie as a superior force who can (as Hurston argues for herself in her autobiography) transcend racism.

The white women are depicted in a double way at the trial. There were a handful present, almost the number of another jury, all with "the pinky color that comes of good food" – pointedly, "nobody's poor white folks" (176). Hurston has Janie yearn for the understanding of these middle-class women, and wish she could tell her story to them "instead of those menfolks" (176). Sexuality and gender appeals here to override class and race. "Love" as a story can translate across class and racial barriers. Hurston is at one with conventional ideology in her emphasis on love conquering all. Or almost all. The white women applaude when the black (male) community is controlled; yet when the verdict of not guilty

103

is rendered, the white women, with happy sentimentality, "cried and stood around her like a protecting wall" (179). These women as women identify with the woman's story of romantic tragedy, no matter the race and class of the protagonists, but identify with their race interests against the African-American males.

Black males – for no black women are *said* to be present except Janie – have the most volatile role. They are fiercely disgruntled that a woman has killed a man, their friend. They repeat, and partially invent, a false story about her adulterous disloyalty, and speak generalizations about the relation of black men and women – even and almost speaking for black women: "No nigger woman ain't never been treated no better [than Janie]" (177). They are also bitter that a woman who "look lak her" has used (as they see it) her gender and color privilege (as looking rather more white than they) to avoid justice. They are ironic on the subject of the cheapness of their lives relative to their race: "[L]ong as she don't shoot no white man she kin kill jus' as many niggers as she please" (179).

Indeed, their conclusion answers Nanny's mule trope at the beginning of the book. Nanny had outlined a stark power hierarchy: "So de white man throw down de load and tell de nigger man tuh pick it up. He pick it up because he have to, but he don't tote it. He hand it to his womenfolks. De nigger woman is de mule uh de world so fur as Ah can see. Ah been prayin' fuh it tuh be different wid you" (14). In contrast, the black men say, "'[U]h white man and uh nigger woman is de freest thing on earth. 'Dey do as dey please" (180). If black women see black women as mules, but black men see black women as free, simple subtraction proposes that the black men are then "de mule(s) uh de world." It is clear to Hurston that their race does not necessarily unify black men and women; they may have different interpretations of their oppression, seeing it distinguished by gender. In the men's terms, a black woman has been elevated into utter powerfulness by killing a black man. It is a disturbing allegation, and shows a bitter conflict of race and gender played out in the black community.

In a sense, the trial scenes multiply. Hurston depicts one trial by white men's hegemonic laws, and one by black men's disgruntled postmortem which Janie overhears from a boarding house room. The white women are a sprinkling of powdered sugar over this confrontation. The black men are wrong, though for some of the right reasons: The political privileges of the white race, of the professional (doctoring, lawyering, judging) class, and of light-colored blacks do exist. The lower-class black men are being done out of their self-proclaimed substitute: their gender privilege, which can include rights of possession, and sexual arousals enforced by light wife-beating and mutual fighting (140, 131–2).[17] And then the white men and women are right for possibly the wrong reasons. Being fascinated by the "whiteness" of this black woman, and by her "romance," but also wanting to put black men in their place, they judge her not guilty. This play of multiple social forces, here visible in the cross-purposed agendas of the two "juries," has the effect of isolating black woman at the intersection point where race, gender, and class and the hegemonic story of romance meet.

The trial of Janie as a black woman does not, however, end with that one complex scene. The whole narrative – Janie's account to her friend Pheoby – is like a trial. The beginning of the novel announces that Janie is being tried by her rural community and condemned without being a "witness" in her behalf, without being asked to testify. The choral collections of folk construct power for themselves through judgment talk, an act that reclaims their humanity despite their being treated as beasts. They scapegoat Janie so they won't themselves be "mules." "Mules and other brutes had occupied their skins. But now the sun and the bossman were gone, so the skins felt powerful and human. They became lords of sounds and lesser things. They passed nations through their mouths. They sat in judgment" (1–2). This rural gossip, with its combination of paralysis and cruelty (depicted at the beginning in the voices of named black women – Pearl Stone, Lulu Moss, Mrs. Sumpkins – and nameless black men), functionally compensates for the speakers' low racial and economic status; at the same time folk tales/folk talk are extremely vital cultural creations. So this folk talk is presented bifocally by Hurston. It is ennobled by the Biblical and ritualized parallelism of the rhetoric in which she presents these gossips, and folk talk is made inadequate by its sour opposition to Janie's value. Janie, then, undergoes a formal trial by the white community, a second informal trial by overhearing black

105

men's bitter aphorisms on her case (179–80), and a third trial by her community of origin. The book involves three trials, one by white people's rules, another by black men's rules, a third by the rules of "Mouth-Almighty" (5) – her black working-class rural community. However, the trial of an autonomous black woman (a black woman who acts equal to anything) cannot play by any of these sets of rules; whatever the judgments rendered, all the trials are inadequate at root. Yet because of the black woman's relative powerlessness, her construction of her own trial by her own rules must be deferred until all of the other trials are finished.

In constructing her story in this way – framed thus, and with key moments of undepicted speech to persons who are only partially equipped to judge (although they have various legal and traditional powers of judgment) – Hurston makes the whole story a "retrial," with the proper jury and judge (a black woman – Pheoby), and the proper witnesses and defense lawyer (all Janie herself; note how in political trials, "criminals" often choose to act as their own lawyers). These trials are temporally lively in the narrative choices Hurston makes. The black female trial (Pheoby and Janie) succeeds higher-class white male and female, lower-class black male, and black community trials chronologically, but envelops them narratively. Therefore, Janie's own self-testamentary trial claims final power and final appeal.

To investigate the whole book as a trial, we must begin with Pheoby.[18] Her very name deserves some comment: It alludes to Diana or Artemis, as luminously bright – but a moon reflecting Janie's sun, for, as Hurston remarks of Janie, "the light in her hand was like a spark of sun-stuff washing her face in fire" (183).[19] A phoebe is also a small dull-colored bird, common in the eastern United States, and distinguished by "its persistent tail-wagging habit."[20] Not only a punning allusion within the book ["you switches a mean fanny round in a kitchen," says Janie to Pheoby (5)], this is also a punning allusion to the power of tale-wagging or storytelling, for Pheoby is invited by Janie to "tell 'em [the gossiping neighbors] what Ah say if you wants to" (6). But Pheoby's first role is to be the jury of her peers which Janie had long sought for a proper (a telling) judgment of her story. As well she is the next (though undepicted) storyteller or tale-wagger: In a striking image

106

of doubled power, Janie remarks: "[M]ah tongue is in mah friend's mouf" (17, cf. *DT* 245), a phrase that means we understand each other so well you could speak for me.

But talk is only one part of power; at novel's end, Janie criticizes those who talk without action: "[L]istenin' tuh dat kind uh talk is jus' lak opening' yo' mouth and lettin' de moon [cf. Phoebe!] shine down yo' throat" (183). Pheoby is not one of the actionless – at least according to her self-proclaimed growth and her vow to make Sam take her fishing. But insofar as tales are substitutes for action, the full weight of Janie's final judgment – for she is judge as well as criminal and lawyer – is levied against that displacement. "Talk" in the deep narrative ideology of this novel can be seen bifocally – as folk power, activated knowledge, and judgment possibly motivating action, or as the powerless substitution for both knowledge and action. This bifocal vision of the "talk" of the porch-sitters is a replica of Hurston's contradictory and subtle notions of race: It is a source of power; yet some use it as a shoddy excuse for powerlessness. Thus Janie's silence, insofar as it was filled with "finding out about livin'" autonomously, with learning the necessity "tuh *go* there to *know* there," and with "going tuh God" (183) – a metaphor for extremes of death, love, and suffering – Janie's thinking silence (keeping inside and outside distinct, having "a host of thoughts" not yet to be expressed, as in the passage on 112–13) is a source of knowledge depicted as equal to her tale wagging.[21]

There are, as Michael Awkward shows, long passages of – long years of – a protesting silence, punctuated with Janie's tart and decisive speech; but these passages – involving gender and sexual silence with her husband, alias "big voice" (43, 75), class silence with the porch-sitting folk – are now "spoken" by Janie. The novel constructs the female hero as narrating her own silences; she is unsilencing them in the specific context of testifying to Pheoby. To appreciate this narrative strategy, I want to look closely at several incidents of what is called undepicted speech. These are moments when Hurston says that Janie spoke, but Janie's speaking is not rendered in Janie's voice when it occurs. The primary moments are on the muck, in the courtroom scene, and with Eatonville's "Mouth-Almighty." On the muck, in the context of all men, the narrative informs us: "The men held big arguments here like they used to do on the store porch. Only here, she could listen and laugh and even talk some herself if she wanted to. She got so she could tell big stories herself from listening to the rest" (127–8). In the courtroom scene (278), Hurston gives a lot of interior motives and notions that Janie was trying to communicate, but about her telling, Hurston simply says: "She just sat there and told and when she was through she hushed" (178). The implication is that her words had a terrific impact. A third important moment of un-depicted speech occurs as the ostracized Janie returns to her community's judgment, characterized as "mass cruelty" (2) by Hurston: "When she got to where they were she turned her face on the bander log and spoke. . . . Her speech was pleasant enough, but she kept walking straight on to her gate" (2). All these undepicted speeches function to "save up" Janie's talk until she has a chosen place and time and audience.

There is a vital ideological meaning for undepicted speech as a narrative strategy. Undepicted speech is Hurston's narrative resolution of conflictual social determinants of race, class, and gender. In a response to the courtroom situation, Hurston depicts Janie actually speaking her tale in and for the black community only, even though the white community is depicted as allowed to hear, and is even seen rendering a better judgment. Thus with the undepicted speech in the courtroom scene, Janie "tells" her tale to whites, but she will later really speak her love story and life narrative to a black person. Hurston thus resolves a tension about power and powerlessness (as it intersects with race), offering Janie's speech back to "the Negro farthest down." But not all these African-Americans appreciate Janie. Because of her explorations of social class and of sexual freedom, they bully her. So Hurston must arrange for this speech to "go" to a black person or persons untainted by authoritarian gossip, for rural "Mouth-Almighty" here brooks comparison with Joe Starks's mercantilist "I God" as a parallel misuse of power, authority, and voice. Janie disparages the community that will not listen (listening, the kind of intimate empathetic listening that Pheoby does, is a requisite for good talk). The porch-sitters who judge her are unlistening talkers already scripting a narrative for her whether or not they have all, or even any, of the proper information (see 5–7). Therefore Hurston will locate Janie's telling to and for one black woman alone, which solves the issue of unlistening community by selecting a listening individual who can represent "the Negro farthest down": a black woman.[22] Hurston chooses a woman listener, which recalls Janie's desire, in the courtroom scene, to speak to white women rather than white men. Similarly, Hurston will make race a factor that intersects with "class" or values of curiosity, mobility, and change by choosing a person (Pheoby) who has separated herself from the porch-sitters. In proposing these moments of undepicted speech, Hurston disassembles three significant groups (race, class, gender), and makes, through narrative choices, subtle distinctions, subtle judgments among them.

2

This novel's title, although clearly generated at one moment in the work, is mysterious in its meaning, not easily glossed in relation to the body of the novel as a whole. Yet even before Pheoby moves toward Janie's house with a covered bowl of mulatto rice, the absolute beginning of the book begins playing with title materials and meanings by opening issues about words and the Word in relation to gender and racial power. The third paragraph starts with a revisionary articulation of Biblical rhetoric "So the beginning of this was a woman" in the place of, taking the world-creating place of Word or God. This woman has seen the "sudden death, their eyes flung wide open in judgment" (1) – making both an allusion to those drowned in the flood, and a prefiguration of the theme of judgment. "Their eyes" is, of course, one portion of the title and a reference to it. All of the moments of special metaphors in the title and elsewhere bear some relation to the multiple social determinants that are narratively active in the novel.

"The sun was gone . . ." (1) and the story begins, at the end of which night, a new sun emerges, and that sun is a woman. Indeed, she appropriates the horizon "from around the waist of the world" for her own garment and gives Tea Cake "the sun for a shawl"

(183). Given the cosmic imagery of the ending – the "fishing for life" (which relocates the different episodes of pleasure, leisure, and fishing in this book) – one might say that the progress or education of the novel is about a black woman who changes from being a mule to being a sun.[23] And being a "sun" is, as Henry Louis Gates points out with a significant citation from *Mules and Men*, related to the ability to "seek out de inside meanin' of words."[24] How do the "inside meanin'[s] of words" act within the novel? How is language susceptible to analysis by feminist cultural studies?

The separation of animal from human by the related acts of talking and judgment is made especially crucial to that being called, in Nanny's monologue, "de mule uh de world" (14): woman. The "Nanny" section of the novel unfolds itself as a doomed dialectic between sexual pleasure and racial prejudice which issues in the enforcing of gender and class protection. Social decency, straight paths, reductions of impulse all are the desired end: Janie, her Nanny decrees, must "marry protection" (14). Protection ironically takes the form of a man; self-sufficiency is not and cannot be a thought, although Nanny herself has, within racial parameters (and with the help of Mrs. Washburn), achieved it. Choice does not enter; but Janie makes a rudimentary sexual–gender resistance to graceless Logan Killicks and his dim rural life (i.e., to class and to race construed in a limited, servile way). In fact, allegorically speaking, this marriage is an image for slavery.[25] It is significant that as she leaves the marriage, Janie was about to become Killicks's third mule and put behind a plow. The kind of economic "protection" offered by the first marriage is explicitly tabulated by Tea Cake much later in the novel as inadequate. Thinking that Janie might need protection (autonomy) from "some trashy rascal" (124), Tea Cake teaches Janie how to shoot. She thereupon becomes a dazzling shot; self-sufficient in this precise way, she is able to protect herself against a most unpredictable and tragic assault, ironically by Tea Cake himself.

Protection as Nanny construes it – gender and class based – is in the most articulate contradiction to sexualities. And Hurston does not stint in our understanding of this by her lavishly sensual and orgasmic description of the pear tree, Janie's own articulation of

110

her desire.²⁶ But that desire, as Nanny then tells, if not innocent and naive, must be informed and infused with the history and genealogy of race told in another tree metaphor: by virtue of slavery, "us colored folk is branches without roots." Under slavery, political power for real social interaction is eradicated: "It sho wasn't mah will for things to happen lak they did" (15), says Nanny. Note the emphasis, even in her utter powerlessness, on bringing things about, making things happen.

What follows is an open-ended narrative of severe sexual as well as socioeconomic bondage for black women. The colonial and class relations working together make of Nanny at once "a work-ox and a brood-sow" (15). The doubling of the animal image makes monstrous the situation, though not the person. Nanny was the favored slave, and bore her master's children; deprived of his protection during his absence in the Civil War, she is threatened by the master's wife in such drastic ways that she flees, despite having just been brought to childbed, of a daughter, Janie's mother.²⁷ That daughter, Leafy (a name in poignant relation to the tree metaphor), was raped at seventeen by her school teacher – a kind of class betrayal, for, as Nanny says, "Ah was 'spectin' to make a school teacher out of her" (36). She never recovered and became troubled and promiscuous. With that racially and socially inflected sexual history as Janie's matrilineage, it is significant that one could read the novel as a quest for autonomous, pleasurable sexual choice – the lessons of Tea Cake cut deeply into the seared and sere terrain of the postslavery generations of black womanhood.

Despite being severely repudiated by Janie ["she hated her grandmother" (85)], Nanny is given a profound narrative and textual function by Hurston. She is the prophet – without honor perhaps, but serving the function of textual prophet. For Nanny's words are predictive and come true later in the novel.²⁸ The creative word, the word acting in time, the word able to bring events into being, is a mighty powerful word. Nanny says the word, and then the word is made flesh and narrative in Janie, who is called, in her incipient state, her grandmother's "text" (16). One might say that Hurston compensates Nanny for typical historical losses in slavery and Reconstruction by endowing her with the power of the word.

111

For instance, Nanny says, "Ah can't die easy thinkin' maybe de menfolks white or black is makin' a spit cup outa you" (19). The sexual vulnerabilities of both grandmother and mother are recapitulated here. That spit cup is suggestively literalized in the Joe Starks section, for he has provided the most up-to-date spittoons his town has ever seen, and the commentary, sotto voce, is made through this text by Hurston – but it's still a spit cup after all; it's a spittoon like the ones whites use in a "bank up there in Atlanta" (44) and it "made the rest of them feel that they had been taken advantage of" (45). This spittoon condenses Joe Starks's class superiority (indeed, his structural "whiteness") and his sexual reductionism in one image.

Probably the most striking metaphor literalized in the text is "de mule uh de world," for the mule as well as spittoon is the sign under which Janie's marriage to Joe Starks unfolds. With Nanny's mule soliloquy as groundwork, the choral comments of the male community pass from Jody and "dat chastisin' feelin' he totes" (46) to the mule. Indeed the men are called "muletalkers" and the mule is the subject – one might say the allegory – they propose. Chapters 6 and 7 contain the climactic analysis and disintegration of Joe and Janie's relationship, interwoven with the fate of the mule. The mule is any and all "underclasses": deprived, overworked, starved; it is the butt of jokes; it is stubborn and ornery to its master, with ways of resistance that are deeply appreciated by the talkers. Indeed: "Everybody indulged in mule talk," says Hurston with devastating clarity. "He was next to the Mayor in prominence and made better talking" (50). The figure of the mule summarizes power relations of class, race, and gender: the porchsitters to Joe, all blacks to whites, and Janie herself to Joe, who, although she had "thought up good stories on the mule," was forbidden to say them. This is the symbol of all the silencings Joe imposes on Janie throughout their marriage, and has been seen as such by most critics of the novel.

Janie's bitter empathy for the mule, expressed in words overheard by Joe, precipitates the striking event of its "emancipation," with its multiple social meanings. "People ought to have some regard for helpless things" (54) is her comment to herself, and it clearly figures her own sense of gender entrapment and speechlessness. Joe responds by purchasing the mule – "Ah bought dat varmint tuh let 'im rest" (54) – a moment of social largesse that can be construed in class terms, as a sign of his superiority to the folks who must work a mule – and themselves – to death. Janie's moving, eloquent response to the "free mule" (55) figures the moment with touching irony as if Starks were the Great Emancipator – a white king who frees the Negroes, in racial noblesse oblige. But Janie's brief speech in Starks's honor precipitates a group realization that "[yo]' wife is uh born orator, Starks. Us never knowed dat befo'" – and foreshadows Janie's devastating assumption of speech in the next chapter. So the mule is an actor in Janie's realization and emancipation.[29]

This is nowhere as clearly seen as in Janie's exclusion from the folk festival made of the mule's funeral. At the ideological center of the novel, the figurative "mule uh de world" (a black woman) has been literalized (as a mule), and has become a condensed figure for black, rural, female resistance, and for folk-pleasures in the parody of power. The power of the mule carnival infuses Janie, who then vocally and publicly doubts her husband's potency, power, and "big voice" (75). This accusation punctures his sexual, political, and even economic power. It is the revenge of the mule.

In the Tea Cake section, Hurston continues to explore the ways in which words and tropes reveal the multiple forces she has at stake in the novel. Tea Cake and Janie marry after a sporty and sexually luxuriant courtship, but class remains an issue. "Jody classed me off" (107), says Janie explaining to Tea Cake that this was not her choice or her desire. But Tea Cake is self-conscious about falling in love with a woman of a better class (more propertied), for he is a day worker, and doesn't hang around with "no high muckty mucks" (118); no one will be surprised to see the literalized Muck of the Lake Okechobee region here verbally prefigured. Janie sees her social class as a burden of internalized repression, preventing her from enacting various desires. She says: "Ah wants tuh utilize mahself all over" (107), a phrase with evident sexual but also social resonance: to know all classes and peoples.

She wants to saturate herself in her people to see, feel, and experience what they are – and what she is. And Tea Cake is "the people."[30] Tea Cake leads, for the most part, a high risk, improvident, charmed and charming life; like the blues he sings, he is "made and used right on the spot" (125). He is one who will "cherish de game" (91), a resonant phrase about risk, love, courtship — and the joie de vivre of the character. He is the very opposite of the bourgeois virtues of Joe ["positions and possessions" (47)], and, if anyone cares to remember him, the rural plod of Killicks. He is playful and urbane (indeed urban in certain of his skills, despite his rural worker status). Hence Janie has, among her three husbands, traveled through an array of available social classes. And Hurston's narrative tests each class for its possibilities of satisfying a woman's life — that is, she tests social class by gender criteria. Reckless gambling artists come out best. Tea Cake gambles with fate; he is, indeed, a gambler, and that gaming quality is a trope for existential risks ultimately respected by Hurston. In fact, she has put some of that in her title, for a roll of the dice during the storm does not abolish chance, but only accentuates it. And in that spirit, the eyes of the gamblers, male and female, watch God.

Janie has, by Tea Cake's actual sincerity, avoided the fate of poor Mis Tyler, taken for the proverbial ride by a young gigolo; this story of her sexual and gender trap is threateningly interwoven throughout the account of their early marriage. Hurston then constructs, with great cunning, a second trap built of the crosscurrents of class and race, with a tricky admixture of gender and sexuality.[31] The long and subtle treatment of Mrs. Turner (Chapters 16 and 17), and the relationship of the names Mis Tyler and Mrs. Turner, indicates that there is some link between the incidents.

Color (and Caucasian features) within race has always been a painful part of African-American heritage — indeed, as part of a worldwide system of racism which has its roots in economic and imperial domination. Ideas of female beauty coincide with, and support, the political hegemonies of dominant race, class, and sexual choice. The section focusing on Mrs. Turner, which is long, repetitive, and interestingly polemical, is a confrontation with the temptation to "class off" to "lighten up" the race (135) by a kind of eugenicist choice of sexual partner, and to try to put distance of manner as well of skin tone and "features" (thin lips, flat buttocks, narrow or pointed nose) between oneself and other blacks.[32] Although African-American, Mrs. Turner is a racist against Negroes: "Ah can't stand black niggers. Ah don't blame de white folks from hatin' 'em 'cause Ah can't stand 'em mahself" (135). Mrs. Turner is described as a "milky sort" (133), her color light, but also a kind of cow sporting her own rabid opinions ["screaming in fanatical earnestness" (136), in Hurston's judgmental phrase]. Tea Cake overhears her; his comment, "Ah been heah uh long time listenin' to dat heifer run me down tuh de dawgs . . ." (137), is a prophetic image literalized in the flood scene in which a confused cow and a vicious dog in combination are the proximate cause of Tea Cake's irrevocable wound. A rabid dog sitting on a burdened, bewildered beast seems to be Hurston's deep allegorical comment on the system of race-inflected social stratification.

Mrs. Turner identifies Janie as an appropriate companion for no quality but her "whiteness," and would see dark Tea Cake as a husband worthy of Janie only if he would cover his darkness with "plenty money" (134). Janie does not say much to Mrs. Turner's monologues – the two are not equally fanatical. But what she says is to the point: "We'se uh mingled people and all of us got black kinfolks as well as yaller kinfolks. How come you so against black?" (135). Mrs. Turner blames the darkness of certain blacks for the existence of racism: "If it wuzn't for so many black folks it wouldn't be no race problem. De white folks would take us [i.e., people of her approximate color] in wid dem. De black ones is holdin' us back" (135). The debate about "Booker T." occurs in this context. There is cultural irony when Mrs. Turner calls him "uh white folks' nigger" (136).[33] Janie claims not to have thought much about this subject, but produces the opinion that class is a greater determinant than race for blacks' position: "Ah don't figger dey [whites] even gointuh want us for comp'ny. We'se too poor" (135).

There are other, subtle ways in which pure racial polarization is disavowed while race is factored in as a deeply structuring social determinant. The plot against Mrs. Turner's restaurant begins with a boycott: "Since she hate black folks so, she don't need our money in her ol' eatin' place. Ah'll pass de word along. We kin go tuh dat white man's place and git good treatment" (137). Of course, the protest ends in an ironically complicit and staged incident, in which Tea Cake, chivalrously defending Mrs. Turner's "niceness" from "dumb niggers" (142), wreaks, with their help, the proper amount of destruction to drive Mrs. Turner back to "civilization." In fact, using sequence tellingly, Hurston opens the next chapter with an exact and political contrast – a scene of what one might call Pan-Africanism, or alliances across the diaspora – the brief mention of the befriending of the Bahamans by Janie and Tea Cake, which brings their dance and music into fruitful relation with the American blacks. Nationality of itself, color of itself, does not necessarily make prejudicial difference, but constructs *appreciable* difference – differences and specificities that one can appreciate (as the Bahamans bring their music into the "mingling" or as a white man's restaurant is more welcoming than one run by a prejudiced black woman). In her text here, Hurston credits, without showing social or rhetorical stress, those (few) whites who get along with blacks.[34] The white doctor "who had been around so long that he was part of the muck" (167) is able quickly to listen to Tea Cake and Janie's stories, diagnose him, promise to try against fact to save him, and finally, after the death, to bear a "good thought" (7) – honest witness – in Janie's favor.

Race, class, and color within race rise in structural and figural importance in the latter part of the book, building toward, and away from, the hurricane. The coming of the storm is foretold by Native American Seminoles, who can read natural signs. Janie does not leave the low ground, the muck, because she does not believe the best judgment of the Seminoles, but rather, lightly, listens to and believes a loosely structured identification with whites and white values. The Seminole message is heard, but denigrated and denied, and the final point in favor of staying on the low ground is that "Indians are dumb anyhow, always were" (147). Hurston makes a dramatic irony of this racial prejudice, and its unthinking faith in the white man and the "bossman's" (150) ability not to let nature overwhelm them – a gross misjudgment of natural and political powers. It is a key moment when the inability to credit the Seminoles' way of "seeking de inside meanin'" of signs, the denial of the interpreting ability of a nondominant group, means disaster.

As the storm worsens and all chances to drive away from the

flooding lake have been lost, Hurston locates the dramatic revelation of her title: "The time was past for asking the white folks what to look for through that door. Six eyes were questioning *God*" (151).[35] Blacks' unthinking dependence on or internalization of white judgment, "readings," or interpretations is abruptly, startlingly addressed. The contrast of white power as a form of political idolatry and fate's (God's) power is the most particularly striking in this version of the title sentence. Overt white power, narratively absent from most of the work, is still constitutive in a racial caste society; to the degree that blacks believe in this power, their interpretative capacities are controlled.

When Hurston says two pages later, "They seemed to be staring at the dark, but their eyes were watching God" (151), the title is totally present in this citation. In it there is an image of reading, reading through, or piercing the darkness (obviously the natural darkness of the storm, but also possibly blackness) to universals of fate. The characters are trying to read their own fortunes. They seemed to be seeing only the dark, or "being in the dark," but their understanding looked through blackness (or darkness) to something more primary. Here an image encompassing race (blackness) seems to give way to universals of awe. Race is transcended.

There are a number of substitutions for God made in this book, usually in the form of big talkers – "Mouth-Almighty" of the rural folk, and "I God" for Joe Starks's comic blasphemous condensation of political and economic power. Mrs. Turner's "color-struck" state, presented as the worship of a (lower case) god, the idol of whiteness, is just one more moment of idolatry. But Hurston is subtle; to some degree all blacks in the book are capable of this kind of idolatry; it is not only externalized in a dismissible character or two, but it also increasingly delimits the choices and judgments of the various and collective heroes. Although in the overlay of meanings clustered in the pages that announce the title, Hurston shifts meaning from race to fate itself, yet still she makes clear that there is no fate in this book uninflected by race.[36] Hence the title is contradictory in its impact. It talks about fate and race at once, and a single meaning cannot be settled one way or the other.

Dramas of race occur in a telling scene when Tea Cake is pressed into service in Palm Beach by two authoritative white men with rifles. The sullen, racially mixed crew is instructed to "examine" the rotting bodies to ascertain which storm victims are white and which are black so they may be differentially buried, the one in coffins, the other in mass graves. However, it is graphically stated, "[D]e shape dey's in[,] can't tell whether dey's white or black" (165). What use is color to ultimate facts: death, fate? Meantime, these dead bodies are described as "watching, trying to see beyond seeing" (162), yet another version of the title phrase. "Watching," then, becomes a way of seeing which gets beyond seeing normally; "normally" here involves seeing difference, especially racial difference. In this use, it appears that Hurston's title is an encoded critique of the color line (whether managed or evoked by white or black) and especially of white power. The human knowledge that the staring dead have is richer and deeper than the mere political prejudices of the whites.

But let me give Tea Cake the final, ambiguous word – ambiguous in its racial notions, and so fully in character and voice that it is hard to decipher: "They's mighty particular how dese dead folks goes tuh judgment . . . Look lak dey think God don't know nothin' 'bout de Jim Crow law" (163). These two statements cut two ways. The first may suggest that God Himself doesn't care about men's laws and exterior differences in judging those brought before Him. (And He is reputed not to.) The second sentence says that these white men are overly scrupulous in preparing segregated facilities for the dead, since God is clearly capable of making Jim Crow separations if He wants to, and even from masses of dead human material buried jointly in one grave. If omnipotent means anything, it certainly means the power to individualize and make distinctions among the putrescent mass. They are acting as if God were a dummy. (And He is reputed not to be.) One sentence mocks white political pretension, whereas the other suggests casually that racial prejudice might have divine approval. In this novel, "God" is evoked mainly as cosmic critique of the lunacies of racist politics; the use of God in the title is an "inside meanin'" that suspects the normative politics of race and power. And thus one might watch Him with awe. But He also might be an image for the implacability of political power, as experienced by African-Americans; God might indeed know too much about the Jim

Crow laws. One might then watch Him warily, bifocally. Even in her denials that race matters, and her invocations of cosmic or color-blind standards, Zora Neale Hurston makes it matter.

NOTES

1. Janie's lightness of skin tone is commented upon at several junctures. Mary Helen Washington remarks that descriptions of Janie draw upon discourses of the "mulatto novel" and its conventions of romance. *Invented Lives: Narratives of Black Women 1860–1960*, ed. Mary Helen Washington (Garden City: Anchor Press, 1987), p. 250. Hurston made this choice despite her insistence that "before being tampered with" by white cultural values (and Northern values), darker Negro women were not disparaged by the folk. Hurston, "Characteristics of Negro Expression," in Nathan Irvin Huggins, *Voices from the Harlem Renaissance* (New York: Oxford University Press, 1976), pp. 233–5.
2. There are a variety of provocative readings of this briefly mentioned, but textually foregrounded, nickname. Among them, Houston A. Baker, Jr., says that the nickname indicates the "marginally situated" Afro-American who has "the possibility of all names" (*Blues, Ideology, and Afro-American Literature* [Chicago: University of Chicago Press, 1984], p. 59); and Henry Louis Gates, Jr., says that Janie is a "nameless child" (*The Signifying Monkey* [New York: Oxford University Press, 1988], p. 185).
3. Hurston, "How It Feels To Be Colored Me" (1928), in *I Love Myself When I am Laughing . . . : A Zora Neale Hurston Reader*, ed. Alice Walker (New York: The Feminist Press, 1979), p. 153.
4. Hurston, *Dust Tracks on a Road: An Autobiography* (1942), second edition, including previously unpublished chapters (Urbana: University of Illinois Press, 1984), p. 330. Subsequently cited as *DT* in text, where needed for clarity. One will not easily forget, among other telling symbolic incidents about the irregular acquisition of education and a relationship to culture, Hurston finding a copy of the *Complete Milton* in the garbage.
5. In *A World of Difference* (Baltimore: Johns Hopkins University Press, 1987), Barbara Johnson discusses this essay: "Far from answering the question of 'how it feels to be colored me,' she deconstructs the very grounds of an answer, replying, 'Compared to what? As of when?

Who is asking? In what context? For what purpose? With what interests and presuppositions?'" (178).

6. The essay dates from 1981, in *The New Feminist Criticism*, ed. Elaine Showalter (New York: Pantheon, 1985), p. 260.

7. In Terry Eagleton's succinct formulation: "[T]he field of discursive practices in society as a whole, [with] particular interest . . . in grasping such practices as forms of power and performance." *Literary Theory: An Introduction* (Minneapolis: The University of Minnesota Press, 1983), p. 205.

8. Nancy Miller, "Arachnologies," in her *Subject to Change: Reading Feminist Writing* (New York: Columbia University Press, 1988), pp. 83–90.

9. Lillian Robinson, "Feminist Criticism: How Do We Know When We've Won?" in *Feminist Issues in Literary Scholarship*, ed. Shari Benstock (Bloomington: Indiana University Press, 1987), p. 147.

10. She even footnotes her use of the term thus: "The word Nigger used in this sense does not mean race. It means a weak, contemptible person of any race." She of course begs the question of the origin of this particular synonym for "contemptible" (*DT* 41).

11. Cora Kaplan, "Pandora's Box: Subjectivity, Class and Sexuality in Socialist Feminist Criticism," in her *Sea Changes: Culture and Feminism* (London: Verso, 1986), pp. 147–176.

12. There may be other of her attitudes, but this gives some of the range. (I cannot here "specify texts, politics, movements" with which these statements are in dialogue, to cite Cora Kaplan, "Keeping the Color in *The Color Purple*" (184), but I would like to note the necessity of doing so.)

13. Robert E. Hemenway, *Zora Neale Hurston: A Literary Biography* (Urbana: University of Illinois Press, 1977), pp. 106–8.

14. Part of Susan Friedman's idea about palimpsest and version, seeing author-repeated stories "as part of an endless web of intertexts": Friedman, "Return of the Repressed in H.D.'s Madrigal Cycle," in *Signets: Reading H.D.*, ed. S. Friedman and R. B. DuPlessis (Madison: University of Wisconsin Press, 1990).

15. Houston A. Baker, Jr., *Modernism and the Harlem Renaissance* (Chicago: The University of Chicago Press, 1987), is the source of this key phrase. He argues that there are two potentially intersecting strategies of Afro-American modernism. The first is "mastery of form" – a "minstrel" mimicry of surface exactness parallel to "white" art as a kind of mask under which folk "sounds" can be given room. The second is "deformation of mastery" – a strategy of display, advertising the engagement of hegemonic cultural training with folk materials to

prepare some fusion of class and mass. Baker, passim, pp. 15–81. For "displacement" and "delegitimation" see DuPlessis, *Writing Beyond the Ending: Narrative Strategies of Twentieth-Century Women Writers* (Bloomington: Indiana University Press, 1985). Both are tactics making critiques of conventional story or narrative, but extended to mean tactics criticizing accepted (hegemonic) modes, manners, and conventions of storytelling.

16. I will not treat reception at all, but production is a point of great interest. For any text has to be made, and the conditions of its making are a tremendous site for feminist investigation, as Virginia Woolf, Tillie Olsen, and Adrienne Rich have all shown in their generative, analytic essays. The forces at work in Hurston's production, including a kind of scholarly sharecropping, have been strikingly and forcefully presented by Robert E. Hemenway.

17. Hurston also constructs a reconciliation between Tea Cake's friends and Janie at the funeral; they knew they were wrong about Janie, and run another of the Turners off the muck as a scapegoat for their feelings of betrayal. But this reconciliation is understated, for it is not part of the political balance sheet Hurston is drawing.

18. This point about the centrality of the trials is similar to a work by Carla Kaplan (Yale University), which I heard after writing this paper; her provisional title is "Negotiating Distance: Zora Neale Hurston and Juridical Narratives."

19. *Dust Tracks* tells us that Hurston lived under the maternal injunction "'Jump at de sun'" (21).

20. Roger Tory Peterson, *A Field Guide to the Birds* (Boston: Houghton Mifflin, 1934), p. 109, *Soyornis phoebe:* "This grey tail-wagger has a weakness for small bridges. . . . This lack of wing-bars, its upright posture, and its persistent tail-wagging are all good points [to facilitate identification]."

21. This comment is meant to enter an ongoing debate about speech and silence in this novel. Feminist analysis has valorized the assumption of voice that characterizes Janie as hero (cf. B. Johnson). African-American critics Robert Stepto and, in reluctant agreement, Mary Helen Washington, have suggested that Janie does not finally achieve a voice. Washington notes that Janie's final comments make "an implicit criticism of the culture that celebrates orality to the exclusion of inner growth" (*Invented Lives*, 247). I have echoed that here. Michael Awkward argues, against Stepto, that part of the point of the novel is Janie's learning to "dislike talk for talk's sake" (59), that Janie exhibits differing relations to talk and action in the course of the

121

novel, and that Janie has learned both "her own voice's authenticating power" and the value of community; hence Hurston offers a narrative strategy that "represents collective interaction rather than individual dictation." See *Inspiriting Influences: Tradition, Revision, and Afro-American Women's Novels* (New York: Columbia University Press, 1989), pp. 53–55.

22. Hurston's pattern of preferring an individual figure as more satisfying than a stereotyped group is visible throughout *Dust Tracks*.

23. Susan Willis, *Specifying: Black Women Writing the American Experience* (Madison: The University of Wisconsin Press, 1987) offers this clarification: "[I]n the black cultural tradition, 'goin' fishn',' fish tales and fish fries commonly suggest 'time off' and the procuring of food by alternative economic means" (p. 9).

24. After a person cites some proverbs, he says, "They all got a hidden meanin', jus' like de Bible. Everybody can't understand what they mean. Most people is thin-brained. They's born wid they feet under de moon. Some folks is born wid they feet on the sun and they kin seek out de inside meanin' of words." *Mules and Men* (Bloomington: Indiana University Press, 1935; reprint, 1963), p. 135. Gates is speaking of signifyin(g) as a skill in interpreting the figurative, pp. 205–6.

25. And Michael Awkward points to the *Starks* marriage as slavery; putting these two together, one might then see *Bildung* in this novel as deeply related to and figuring Emancipation, and this despite Hurston's presenting slavery, in *Dust Tracks*, as having occurred in the past and being of no particular concern to her.

26. Later matured, beyond this tree of heterosexual romance to the tree of life where "[d]awn and doom was in the branches" (20). A rich and complete tracing of this tree metaphor is found in Gates, *Signifying Monkey*.

27. Houston Baker offers the most succinct reminder: Under slavery "the owner's sexual gratification (forcefully achieved) was also his profit," for his children were also his property. See *Blues*, p. 57.

28. Both Tea Cake and Janie have at least one such prophetic moment; Nanny has several. Many of her words are brought into action.

29. Early in the Starks section, upon the couple's arrival in Eatonville, Janie is asked for a brief speech, a suggestion abruptly cut off by Joe. Not only a prefiguration of the silencing of the bourgeois woman ["she's uh woman and her place is in de home" (69)], it also suggests that the folk have an easier and more tolerant relationship to female speech.

30. So much so that I argued in *Writing Beyond the Ending* that their

Power, Judgment, and Narrative

relationship was less romance for its own sake than the expression of a quest for community.

31. Tea Cake, first in jest and then in desperate seriousness, attempts to suspect that Janie is going to desert him for Mrs. Turner's brother.

32. Indeed, Missy Dehn Kubitschek points out that "[e]ach community in the novel – that of Nanny, Eatonville, and Belle Glade – contains a black character or a group of black characters who have internalized white values." "'Tuh de Horizon and Back': The Female Quest," in *Modern Critical Interpretations: "Their Eyes Were Watching God,"* ed. Harold Bloom (New York: Chelsea House, 1987), p. 31.

33. There could be more to say about this glancing allusion to Booker T. Washington. As a partial context, Hurston's opinion, in *Dust Tracks*, was that Washington was wrongfully considered a pariah by upwardly mobile African-Americans for "advocating industrial education" – a reminder of lower class and racial status which certain blacks tried to ignore; p. 233.

34. *Dust Tracks* makes the same point about black and white in a more overt and staged fashion, as I have indicated above.

35. Janie and Tea Cake have been joined by a friend, hence the six eyes.

36. See, for example: "[W]hite folks had preempted that point of elevation and there was no more room" (243) for others in their escape from the flood.

123

Notes on Contributors

Michael Awkward is an Associate Professor who teaches in the English Department and the Center for Afro-American and African Studies at the University of Michigan. He is the author of *Inspiriting Influences: Tradition, Revision, and Afro-American Women Novelists* (1989).

Hazel Carby, Professor of English and African-American Studies at Yale University, is the author of *Reconstructing Womanhood: The Emergence of the Afro-American Woman Novelist* (1987). She is working on a study of twentieth-century African-American women's cultural production.

Rachel Blau DuPlessis is Professor of English at Temple University. She is the author of *Writing Beyond the Ending: Narrative Strategies of Twentieth-Century Women Writers* (1985), *H.D.: The Career of That Struggle* (1986), and *The Pink Guitar: Writing as Feminist Practice* (1990); and the editor of *The Selected Letters of George Oppen* (1990).

Robert Hemenway is the author of *Zora Neale Hurston: A Literary Biography* (1977). Formerly the Dean of Arts and Sciences at the University of Oklahoma, he has recently been appointed Chancellor at the University of Kentucky.

Nellie McKay is Professor of Afro-American and American Literature at the University of Wisconsin. The author of *Jean Toomer, Artist* (1984) and editor of *Critical Essays on Toni Morrison* (1988), she is currently working on a study of twentieth-century Afro-American women's autobiographies.

Selected Bibliography

The text of *Their Eyes Were Watching God* for this volume is from Perennial/Harper and Row (1990). The University of Illinois Press's edition (first produced in 1978), had been for some time the only version of Hurston's novel available. Illinois's edition, which is the form through which most contemporary readers were introduced to the novel, is now out of print. Along with the books and essays cited in the notes of this volume's essays, the reader may wish to consult studies in the following selected bibliography.

Awkward, Michael. *Inspiriting Influences: Tradition, Revision, and Afro-American Women Novelists.* New York: Columbia University Press, 1989.

Baker, Houston A., Jr. *Blues, Ideology, and Afro-American Literature: A Vernacular Theory.* Chicago: University of Chicago Press, 1984.

Benesch, Klaus. "Oral Narrative and Literary Text: Afro-American Folklore in *Their Eyes Were Watching God,*" *Callaloo* 11 (Summer 1988): 627–35.

Bethel, Lorraine. "'This Infinity of Conscious Pain': Zora Neale Hurston and the Black Female Literary Tradition," in *But Some of Us Are Brave,* ed. Gloria T. Hull, Patricia Bell Scott, and Barbara Smith. Old Westbury, NY: The Feminist Press, 1982, pp. 176–88.

Brown, Lloyd W. "Zora Neale Hurston and the Nature of Female Perception," *Obsidian* 4 (Winter 1978): 39–45.

Callahan, John. *In the African-American Grain: The Pursuit of Voice in Twentieth-Century Black Fiction.* Urbana: University of Illinois Press, 1988.

Christian, Barbara. *Black Women Novelists: The Development of a Tradition 1892–1976.* Westport, CT: Greenwood Press, 1980.

Cooke, Michael G. *Afro-American Literature in the Twentieth Century: The Achievement of Intimacy.* New Haven: Yale University Press, 1984.

Gates, Henry Louis, Jr. *The Signifying Monkey: A Theory of Afro-American Literary Criticism.* New York: Oxford University Press, 1989.

Hemenway, Robert. *Zora Neale Hurston: A Literary Biography.* Urbana: University of Illinois Press, 1977.

Holloway, Karla F. C. *The Character of the Word: The Texts of Zora Neale Hurston.* Westport, CT: Greenwood Press, 1987.

Howard, Lillie. *Zora Neale Hurston.* Boston: G. K. Hall, 1980.

Howard, Lillie. "Nanny and Janie: Will the Twain Ever Meet?" *Journal of Black Studies* 12 (Winter 1982): 403–14.

Hurston, Zora Neale. *Dust Tracks on a Road: An Autobiography,* ed. Robert Hemenway. 1942. Urbana: University of Illinois Press, 1984. Reprint.

Jordan, Jennifer. "Feminist Fantasies: Zora Neale Hurston's *Their Eyes Were Watching God,*" *Tulsa Studies in Women's Literature* 7 (Spring 1988): 105–17.

Johnson, Barbara. *A World of Difference.* Baltimore: Johns Hopkins University Press, 1987.

Krasner, James. "The Life of Women: Zora Neale Hurston and Female Autobiography," *Black American Literature Forum* 23 (Spring 1989): 113–26.

Kubitschek, Missy Dehn. "'Tuh De Horizon and Back': The Female Quest in *Their Eyes Were Watching God,*" *Black American Literature Forum* 17 (Fall 1983): 109–15.

McCredie, Wendy. "Authority and Authorization in *Their Eyes Were Watching God,*" *Black American Literature Forum* 16 (Spring 1982): 25–8.

Meese, Elizabeth. *Crossing the Double-Cross: The Practice of Feminist Criticism.* Chapel Hill: University of North Carolina Press, 1986.

Pondrom, Cyrena N. "The Role of Myth in Hurston's *Their Eyes Were Watching God,*" *American Literature* 58 (1986): 181–202.

Pryse, Marjorie. "Zora Neale Hurston, Alice Walker, and the 'Ancient Power' of Black Women," in *Conjuring: Black Women, Fiction, and Literary Tradition,* ed. Marjorie Pryse and Hortense J. Spillers. Bloomington: Indiana University Press, 1985, pp. 1–24.

Spillers, Hortense J. "A Hateful Passion, a Lost Love," in *Feminist Issues in Literary Scholarship,* ed. Shari Benstock. Bloomington: Indiana University Press, 1987, pp. 181–207.

Stepto, Robert. *From Behind the Veil: A Study of Afro-American Narrative.* Urbana: University of Illinois Press, 1979.

Walker, Alice. *In Search of Our Mothers' Gardens: Womanist Prose.* San Diego: Harcourt Brace Jovanovich, 1983.

Wall, Cheryl. "Zora Neale Hurston: Changing Her Own Words," in *American Novelists Revisited: Essays in Feminist Criticism,* ed. Fritz Fleischmann. Boston: G. K. Hall, 1982, pp. 371–89.

Wallace, Michele. "Who Dat Say Who Dat When I Say Who Dat?: Zora Neale Hurston Then and Now," *The Village Voice Literary Supplement* (April 1988): 18–21.

Selected Bibliography

Washington, Mary Helen. *Invented Lives: Narratives of Black Women 1860–1960.* Garden City, NY: Doubleday, 1987.

Walker, S. Jay. "Zora Neale Hurston's *Their Eyes Were Watching God:* Black Novel of Sexism," *Modern Fiction Studies* 20 (Winter 1974–5): 519–28.

Weixlmann, Joe, and Baker, Houston A., Jr., eds. *Studies in Black American Literature 3: Black Feminist Criticism and Critical Theory.* Greenwood, FL: Penkevill Publishing, 1988.

Willis, Susan. *Specifying: Black Women Writing the American Experience.* Madison: University of Wisconsin Press, 1987.

Wolff, Maria Tai. "Listening and Living: Reading and Experience in *Their Eyes Were Watching God,*" *Black American Literature Forum* 16 (Spring 1982): 29–33.